Memory Improvement

Gain Accelerated Learning Capabilities to Increase Concentration and Memory and Remember More

By: Adam Goleman

Disclaimer Notice.

Please note the information contained within this document is for educational and entertainment purpose only. This book not intended to be a substitute for medical advice. Please consult your health care provider for medical advice and treatment.

Table of Contents

Chapter4: Memory Improvement Techniques

Chapter5: What is a Photographic Memory?

Introduction

Congratulations on purchasing your copy of the book *Memory Improvement: Gain Accelerated Learning Capabilities to Increase Concentration and Memory and Remember More,* and thank you for doing so.

The following chapters will discuss the intricate world where thoughts reside, memories are built, and cognition rejuvenates. Your mind is a whole universe compacted in a small area. The nature of nervous paths interconnecting the brain regions define the way you behave, think, act, and memorize. The traces left by the passage of bio-electric signals on this path make up your memory structures. The more the similar path is visited or revisited, the more defined and prominent the traces will be and the stronger your memories will become. However, the theory suggests that these traces tend to fade away over time due to one or many reasons. There may be a lack of proper brain diet and workout, or inadequate sleep, or perhaps a lack of reconnections and regular revisions.

Lost focus, will power, and concentration can also be the reason for memory decline so that it can be the weakened state of biochemical energy inside the body. Let us explore these reasons and their solutions in the upcoming chapters. Are you eager to know some of the most effective techniques for memory improvement and accelerated learning? Embark on this exciting reading ride to review these strategies and be aware of how to maintain your mental health properly.

Books about the subject are aplenty in the market, we appreciate that you picked this one! Every energy spent on creating this book was focused on giving as much useful information as entertaining. Have a happy reading!

Chapter 1: Memory in Our Mind

Humans are thinking animals. The more we see and observe, the more experiences we gain, and thus more memories are made in our minds. But the question is, what actually is considered as memory?

What is Memory?

Being a part of a social environment, we are living numerous experiences on a day to day basis. Think of them as packets or blocks of raw data that enter the cognitive arena and get decoded by the mind. Now this decoded information, once comprehended, becomes a sensible memory and is stored in a file inside the brain to access at a later stage.

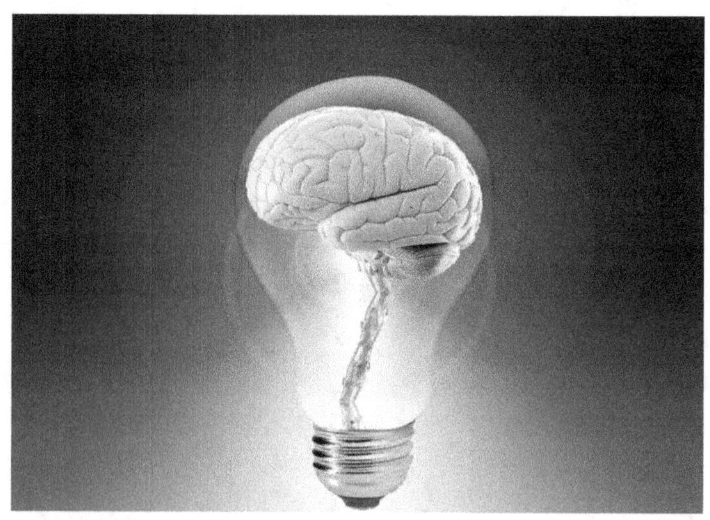

The Brain as a Memory Storage

Consider our brain; it is a powerhouse of several processes running cognitively, including perception, listening, thinking, and talking. Among these processes, memory analysis is also a very important intellectual process. By saving memories as imaginary files organized according to the priority level and retrieval redundancy, our mind works systematically. How are memories triggered? It depends on a kind of familiar environment or a certain object to which a person is exposed. As we try to recall, our mind accesses the respective memory file in the virtual storage cabinets and retrieves it so that a particular scenario or event is refreshed in mind.

Structure of the Mind: Synapses or Wiring Connections

The mind has special areas dedicated to processing special functions. Each area or region has some wired connections or synapses that are formed through an ongoing process. It is known that at the time of birth, the human brain is an immature organ, i.e. not fully developed at that time. The development of the brain continues even after birth as the synaptic connections are made and remade. A synapse of a synaptic connection is basically a linkage between neurons through which sensory impulses are passed to conduct a message to the brain center of that region. If these links or channels are frequently used, the connections sustain. However, if the frequency of action is absent, the synaptic connection is weakened, broken, or *pruned.* This ability of the brain to shape and reshape is subjected to the nature of usage and frequency of an action.

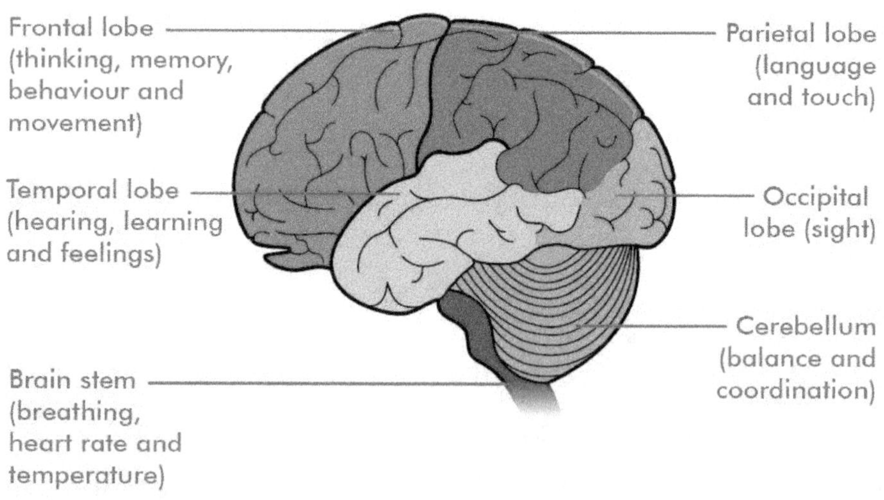

Consider an example of a hearing experience that a person gained earlier. He heard a word; "comprehension". He learned it by hearing as the neurons in the hearing region transmitted the message to the brain through a synapse. Now, if this person frequently hears this word in daily conversations, he will be able to recognize it instantly because the connection is still wired in the brain. But if he doesn't hear or use it for a long time, the connection will be broken. So, the next time he hears that particular word, he wouldn't be able to recognize it instantly as new wiring of connection will have to be formed then. That is why learning new languages become easier through frequent practice and speech.

According to neurologists, the brain has a massive number of wired connections and even though the neurons or brain cells are in a fixed number (i.e. approximately 100 billion neurons), every single neuron is connected to another neuron by numerous synaptic links. The plentitude of synaptic connections, however, doesn't guarantee the brainpower. Instead, the lack of practice and stimulation can easily weaken these connections. The wiring of the brain is actually a network of pathways that should have active signals in order to strengthen the roads or else they could be eliminated. If all the connections are used purposefully, frequently, and systematically, a sort of functional coordination occurs where each action of a person is in sync with the other.

To understand this, consider another example of the facet of language and proficiency i.e. listening, writing, reading, and speaking. If you are listening to a particular story or conversation, your brain cells or neurons will need a pathway to transmit chemical messages or impulses that are carried by sensory messengers called neurotransmitters. They reside in the narrow pathways or passages called synapses which enable the neurons to link together and communicate.

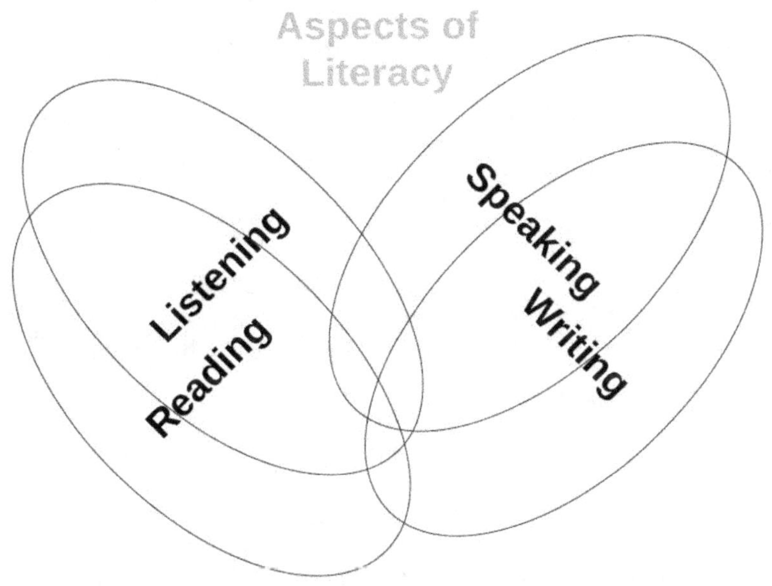

Now, this communication helps in sending the message to the brain and stimulating the desired response, which in this case is the comprehension of the conversation heard. As there is a difference between hearing and listening, the latter requires comprehending the words as well. So, when you have understood what you have heard, listening is completed. But the connection remains there unless a long gap occurs without repeating the action of listening to a similar story or conversation. If you proceed systematically while involving all aspects of literacy learning, you will be able to speak what you have listened and when you do so, a new connection is formed as the neurons involved in the speech region of the brain pass the electrical signals or sensory impulses to it, and this stimulates an utterance or speech in response. While you speak the same words you have listened to, the connections are coordinated, and the response is much faster due to the easy availability of interlinked pathways of synaptic connections.

Afterward, when you start reading the things you have listened to and spoken of, yet another network of wired pathways are generated to transmit the new knowledge to the brain and process it. As the information has already been processed before in the alternative forms of listening and speaking, the reading becomes more familiar and previous knowledge is easier to recall through old connections. Similarly, when you begin to write about what you have learned so far through different aspects of language and literacy i.e. listening, speaking, and reading, you gain a stronger grip on your memory, comprehension, and depth of knowledge due to the good coordination of the miraculous network of wiring present inside your ordinary-looking brain. Therefore, it can be deduced that no one has a good or bad, strong or weak memory. Instead, it goes down to the very fact that how the connections inside our brain are arranged and how with some determined practice, systematic conditioning, and strategic mindfulness, they can be rearranged.

Memory as a Cognitive Process

Among the most intriguing cognitive research debates is the concept of memory as a part of analytical processes running in the human mind. How the mind receives information, processes it and stores it is an intricate, speedy work that may seem ordinary at a superficial glance. However, the mysteries of the brain suggests having a closer look at the whole process to understand it further.

How we learn things depends primarily on our memory. The way we act, the way we behave and exhibit emotions, are all linked to the past memories we have accumulated inside our cognition as indicators or models of future behavior. As Rick Warren quoted: "Your self is created by your memories, and your memories are created by your mental habits." So, our actions can reflect our memories. Hence the importance of improving the memory to improve the present actions and comprehend experiences.

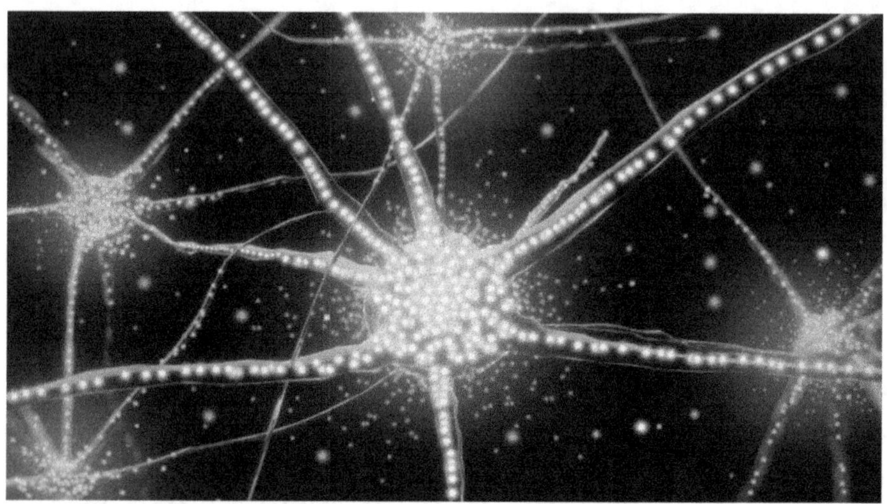

Research shows that in the early years the ability of the brain to learn and relearn i.e. its plasticity is more evident. Young ones are quick to catch new vocabulary, recall words and incidents, and relive past experiences. However, adults too, through practical methods and proven strategies, can clearly improve their memory power and brain performance. These learning strategies and accelerated memory techniques will be further explored in the upcoming chapters.

Surely, you would have often heard a phrase; *"food for thought"*. This could be taken in quite a literal sense as we speak of brain development and memory. In later chapters, you will come to know how our mind needs concentration, purpose and positive experiences to feed on. Just like our body needs vital nutrition and memory-boosting ingredients to gain strength. All of these factors influence our overall performance.

Four Stages of Memory Process

Considering the human mind as an input processing or computing device, the following stages of the memory process can be analyzed comprehensively.

1. **Attention:** At this stage, the person is paying attention to the surroundings or a particular object, event, word, action of interest. This is an observational stage, i.e. perceiving and exploring in detail.

2. **Encoding:** At this stage, the observed facts are taken as input data to be processed in mind. This is a stage of knowledge acquisition. Gaining insights, increasing the intellect and learning new things.

3. Storage: Here the processed information is retained. Storing the encoded experiences helps enables the mind to recall it whenever needed. Therefore this stage is also very important in ensuring the ability of a brain to sustain and prolong learning and comprehension.

4. Retrieval: After the brain has stored the specific information in the respective compartment or functional region, it recovers it when the need for recall arises.

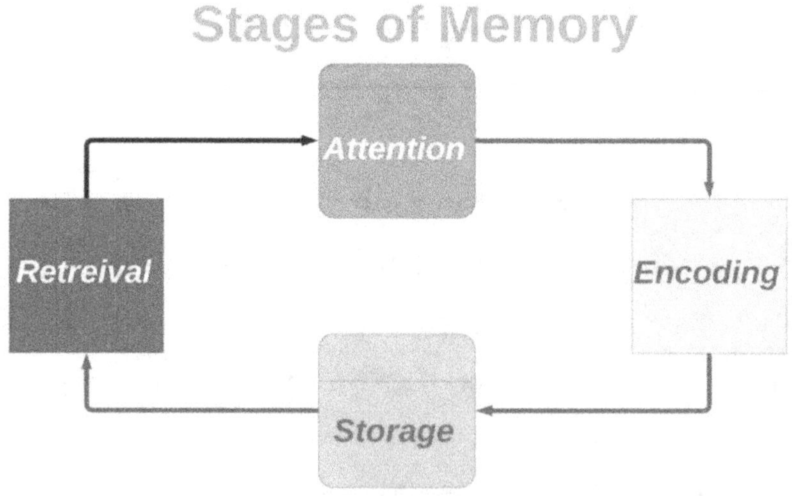

All these four stages of the memory process are equally important.

However, the early practices and research studies focused more on storage and retrieval than on the former two i.e. Attention and Encoding. The modern findings in cognitive research emphasize the need for conscious concentration and focused attention in order to receive information. This is essential for increasing the chances of retention for an extended period of time.

For occasions like these, if a person doing a picture description activity pays close attention to the picture of a park that is shown to him, he is likely to encode the details and objects depicted in the park more effectively.

When he is assessed later, upon being asked comprehensive questions such as; *"What objects would you normally find in a park?"* or, *"What game were the two children in the picture playing?"* or, *"Where was the cat sitting in the park?"*

He is able to recall with more clarity and can answer confidently such as; *"You would normally find benches, play equipment, grassy area, hedges, fences, a fountain, and trees, etc. in a park."* or, *"The two children in the picture were playing catch with a green colored ball."* or,

"The cat, which was black in color, was sitting beneath the corner bench in the park."

How our memory works, how it is retained, and how it is recalled or recovered, can be greatly influenced by the information-processing theories and models that we are following and implementing. In some models or theories, the linkage between the sensory processes of attention and memory retention is so strong that it has been declared as a key to powerful learning and accelerated improvement in the memory retrieval process.

The major details and workings of memory retention and storage will be discussed extensively in the next chapter under the topic; types of memory.

Chapter2: Types of Memory and Memory Loss

The human memory, more appropriately perceived as a process rather than a thing, has 3 distinctive types, which in turn, can be further classified into subtypes. These three types are *sensory memory, short term or working memory, and long-term memory.*

Most often what we refer to as memory in routine life is long term memory. The interesting fact is that the other types of memory like sensory memory and short term or working memory are referred more in terms of their weakness called forgetfulness. However, all these types of memories and their capacity range are important indicators or measures of a person's overall intelligence.

The Sensory Memory

The sensory memory is an instantaneous memory retained or less than a second. Shortest of the three, the sensory memory is used by our senses or sensory organs such as eye, nose, ear, tongue, hands, etc., to take in information from the surrounding environment. The information quickly transferred to the short-term memory registers after being input by the sensory receptors.

There are several things we see, hear, taste, touch, or smell in our daily life, such as a bus passing, a bird flying, smell of coffee brewing, smell of roses while passing by a rose garden, hearing students' chatter while passing by a school building, experiencing roughness upon touching a scrub, tasting bitterness when swallowing medicine. These instances are retained for a short period. The types of sensory memory include visual (iconic) and echoic (audio) memory.

Sensory memory teaches us that information must be coming in small bits in a steady pattern to be manageable and easily transferrable to the short-term memory. Also called sensory register, the sensory memory lays the foundation for short term and long-term memory as without the presence of the former the latter two cannot be formed. That is the main reason senses are called *windows to the mind.* Remember that sensory memory requires paying attention in order to make productive use of your senses. If during a lecture, you are looking outside the class, observing the school grounds. You are exhausting your sensory receptors of both the visual and auditory senses by trying to focus on two directions simultaneously. Now, whichever thing interests you more, or you pay attention to it more, will win a place in the sensory register and you will lose focus on the lecture or tune it out.

Short Term Memory

Being labeled as working memory, it is the part of the memory process where the recently encoded information stays for a short while to be actively used while working presently. All the information processing occurs here, it is a temporary container or notepad for holding the information you are currently working on. It is, therefore, also called primary or active memory. You can perceive short term memory as *RAM* of the mind. In order to retain short term memory, repetitions are needed. You can remember a particular sentence that you have just read for less than a minute before it vanishes from your mind unless you repeat it again.

Memory Consolidation

Memory consolidation is the technique that lets us retain short term memories or prolonged duration. It is the method that basically transforms the short-term memory into long term memory by means of reinforcement and systematic revisions.

Long Term Memory

Long term memory is where our major life experiences are stored in and retrieved from. The storage does not occur in the short-term memory because of its volatile nature. The information in long term memory, however, can be retained for an indefinite duration and can be managed or manipulated. The experiences that you have encountered days before, you can easily recall due to your long-term memory. Major unconscious and conscious decisions in your life are made based on your long-term memory content. The long-term memory can be divided into two important subtypes; *explicit, and implicit memory.*

Explicit Memory

Also called, a conscious memory or declarative memory, an explicit memory type is an objective type of memory that recalls conscious events that are more tangible in nature. These events can either be *episodic* in nature such as past incidents or experiences that you have observed or felt, or *semantic* in nature such as science concepts learned in the class or general world facts that you know of.

Implicit Memory

Implicit memory is more subtle in nature, sort of unconscious. You can recall some procedures without deliberate effort, by way of unconsciously following what you already know. For example, some tasks and procedures are so strongly engraved in your mind that you can follow the steps even with your eyes closed, such as washing dishes, operating a TV remote while your eyes are on the screen, opening your door lock, etc. You perform these tasks daily; these procedures have become familiar patterns of information in your mind and can be recalled unconsciously or automatically. Implicit memory is also called procedural memory.

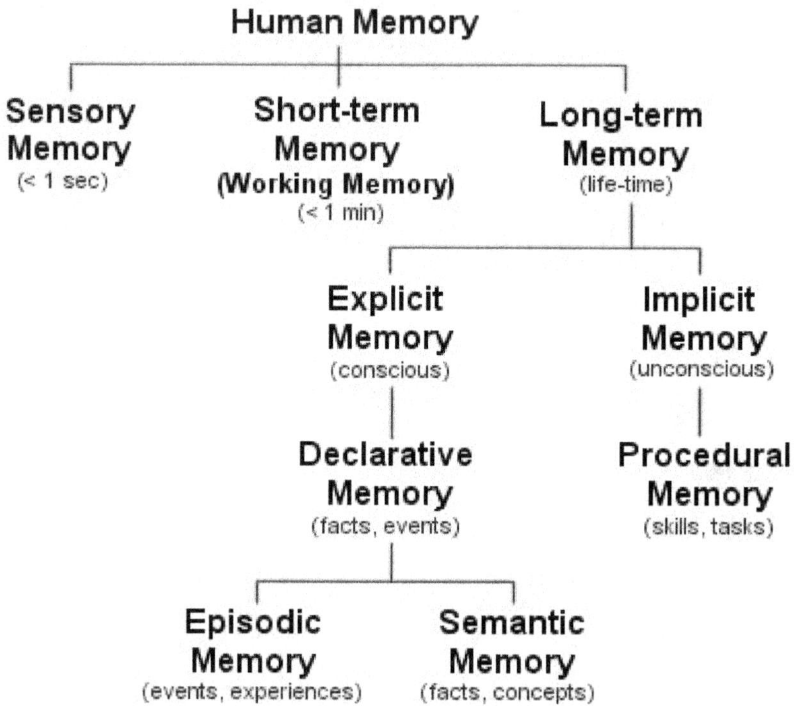

Types of Memory Loss

Memory loss also referred to as *amnesia,* is the neurological phenomena of either an inability to remember or retrieve the information that was stored previously inside the brain or an inability to store new information inside the brain. Certain drug maltreatment, or traumatic experiences, or brain injury or infarction, or extreme seizures due to stress, or excessive alcohol intake, etc. can cause memory loss. Memory loss or amnesia has three major types:

1. Retrograde Amnesia: This type of memory loss causes an inability to remember pre-accident incidents and facts while the person is able to store and recall current memories after the accident.

2. Anterograde Amnesia: This type of amnesia causes the lack of ability to formulate memories of new incidents that have been occurring after the memory loss event i.e. post amnesic incidents. The person suffering from this type of memory loss can remember the past memories though. Alzheimer's, a neurological disease, falls under this category.

3. Global Amnesia:

It is a transient or temporary state of memory loss. It is a combined form of the other two types of amnesia. This is mostly caused by severe stress or sudden shock or concussion. Although quicker to be recovered, it may disrupt the short-term memory for a while. A person should gain adequate rest, relaxation, mental and physical training, to avoid the risk of possible amnesic episodes.

What is Dementia?

To put it in simpler terms, Dementia is an umbrella term for loss of cognitive skills such as thinking, memorizing, comprehending, analyzing, etc. Dementia is often caused by the death of healthy brain cells, due to which normal functioning of the brain is affected. Often it is seen in old-age people who lose even the basic brain functionality in a severe case of the disorder and become dependent on others. Sometimes it is genetic too.

The Decay Theory

The decay theory suggests that memory will fade out with the passage of time. The word decay is supposed to imply that like every tangible matter on earth, time leaves its effect on the memory too, decaying it after a period of time. In an intangible sense, we can say that if left unattended, memory can become replaceable. The explanation of leaving the memory unattended is that memory must be either recalled and remembered from time to time or it gets buried under heaps, and heaps of other relatively new memories. This burial can cause it to decay just like any other matter on earth.

Contrastingly, the interference theory of forgetting states that an interfering thought about a thing can make us lose focus and forget the other things. The decay theory doesn't present the memories to be dependent on each other, instead, it makes them individually dependent on the frequency of recall function.

Chapter3: Mind as a Stack

In a literal sense, a stack is a collection of some items organized one after the other. According to the computer science concept, a stack is a dynamic data structure used to store information in a linear sequence. The stack is so-called because of its resemblance to the stack of plates being added or removed, sequentially starting from the very top going linearly down. The action of *push* and *pop* demonstrates the addition or removal of an element in the stack. It is called dynamic data structure due to its ability to keep changing each time the new information is added or retrieved. The stack works on the principle of *last in first out (LIFO).* This means that the topmost information is the last one to be added but the first one to be removed due to the specific structural nature of the stack data.

There can be a striking resemblance to our mental structure with the stack data structure. The fact that memories in our minds are organized in compartments or cabinets is actually an explanation of the stack concept. The memory cabinets are like filing systems labeled and organized as data structures. Each time a new memory is added, it is pushed upon an existing pile of memories. Each time the same or another memory has to be retrieved, it is removed from the pile linearly.

However, our mind can work both ways i.e. *LIFO (last in first out) as well as FIFO (first in first out).* The first method may be possible if the present working memory is weaker than the long-term old memories. As happens with most patients suffering from dementia. The recent memories are unable to be retained but the old memories are permanently stored and easily retrieved. The second method suggests that the short-term memory is stronger and can retain the newly added information effortlessly to ensure instantaneous retrieval without going to comb through the stacking memories linearly.

The chaos may occur when some of the disturbing memories don't get a proper filing place in the cabinets due to weak memory consolidation or decreased focus during encoding and processing. This has to be programmed systematically. Repeated practice is needed using techniques involving dedicated concentration for memory retention. Before discussing the memory retention and memory improvement techniques or methods, let us first explore the subtle yet important differences between these two targets set by most people for achieving brainpower.

Memory Retention v/s Memory Improvement

Consider the case of Sam, a young man who shares his experience and thoughts on the subject of memory. He says that he believes himself to have an average memory and needs to understand the reason why compared to his peers, he needs a longer time span to memorize things. He also seems worried about his upcoming competitive exam and would like to ensure that he remember things for a longer time period. Sam says that forgetfulness would be a major concern in the exam. So, what is happening? What made him think that he has a weaker memory than his peers? What could the reason behind the *inability to quickly recall recently learned information* and the reason behind the *inability to learn things quickly?*

Memory Retention: Ability to *continue remembering* things that were already learned for a longer time period i.e. *retaining it*.

Memory Improvement: Ability to *quickly memorize things* while learning them.

Coming back to Sam's thoughts, he thinks that the reason why he is unable to memorize things quickly is his lack of belief in his own memory ability. He also cannot recall things as fast as his peers because of his lack of confidence that *he can do it if he wants to do it.* He finds himself doubting the learned facts at the time of quizzes and thus his mind also loses focus and confidence in recalling the things.

Experts say that Sam can have an improved memory when he becomes well-focused. If a person can feel himself to be more confident or rather more focused because of a good memory, he can also have a good memory due to increased confidence. The concept of confidence here is used interchangeably with mental focus.

Memory Reconstruction

This phenomenon suggests that memory can be recalled by way of formulating old experiences on the newer incidents. Many factors such as mental schemas, time, learning attitude, mental inclination, etc., can help alter our memories or reconstruct them. This idea indicates that memory retrieval is often not accurate and can be manipulated. The possibility of a reconstructive memory gives an answer to the questions regarding memory distortion and lack of memory retention. Reliving the past events require a repetition of various mental processes in the brain's working memory. Perception, reasoning, thinking, analysis, etc. The reconstruction process often involves the supplementation of a past memory by using similar experiences and practices that aid in recalling the past memory. These supplementary incidents initiate a cohesive thinking process that enables successful recall.

Several memory-strengthening methods are used to ensure memory errors such as *confabulation* during a recall can be avoided. A confabulated memory can be a falsely fabricated memory without a conscious realization. This normally happens due to a lack of clarity at the time of encoding the information, thus blurring out the events stored with the passage of time. This cognitive dysfunction can be avoided by systematic remembrance of stored information inside the brain. The hippocampus, a small yet essential organ present inside the brain's medial temporal lobe, is the key function center for memory encoding and recall. Experts claim that the hippocampal memory retrieval can transition from recall to reconstruction as more time passes as lack of revision causes the original traces to fade away. Without further ado, let's study some of the most effective memory improvement techniques that can help encode, store, retain, and recall the learned information better, and yes, exactly in that particular order.

Chapter4: Memory Improvement Techniques

Cognitive/Strategic techniques for memory power and enhancement

- <u>**Memory Palace or Magnetic Memory Method**</u>

Also called the method of loci, the memory palace is an amazing tool to increase spatial awareness and visualization power which, in turn, help improve the memory power. As early as the time of Greek civilization, a long history of neurological improvement methods shows the successful use of this method by ancient people.

The method involves the use of imagination and visual creativity. It has been used by popular authors as an interesting plot device in their mystery thrillers as well. To apply this method;

✓ Suppose an imaginary place inside your mind.

- ✓ The more familiar the place, the better. For example, your childhood playground, or your treehouse, or your old town library, or your current home's lounge.

- ✓ The chosen place should be spacious enough to let you store sufficient information. Its details should be clear enough to you in order to visualize with clarity.

- ✓ Decide a specific way of entering and walking through the place. Fix a route or track. Keep that in mind.

- ✓ Now the most important step is to locate the areas or corners of the place where information storage could be possible in your imagination.

- ✓ Consider the data you have to memorize and recall, according to the size of the data, select locations and allocate specific bits of information to them.

- ✓ The spots allocated should be unique and distinguishable, so that information stored wouldn't get mixed up causing unnecessary confusion.

- ✓ Attempt to sketch out your imagined memory palace on a paper to match with your visualization in a more concrete form. Try to get each detail straight.

✓ Select the order for memory allocation, and recall. Recite that order until you get it straight.

✓ Both room or a road can be imagined as a memory palace, use noticeable pieces of furniture, bookshelves, and wall hangings as data allocation spots in case of the former. Whereas, in the case of the latter, select signposts or symbolic landmarks for specific data storage spots.

✓ Distribute your information in small chunks, allocating them to specific locations.

✓ The allocation should be in the order in which you would later retrieve them.

✓ The multiple interesting ways in which the data allocation can be done in your memory palace will be discussed in some subtopics below.

✓ Experts recommend dedicating some time to your memory palace daily. Visualize the place, walk through it, associate the important chunks you need to remember with the specific locations present in your memory place.

✓ The most satisfying aspect of this technique is the ability to practice visualizing the memory bits with your eyes closed, anytime, anywhere.

Another brilliant tip for long term usage is the regular cleaning of the memory palace. This method is reusable over and over again. Your memory palace is quite dynamic and alterable. Use it again by deleting the previous data that is no longer needed for memorization (for instance, after an exam), and reallocate newer information inside the same place.

The memory palaces can be used extensively in a variety of subject areas to memorize and retain key information. Memorizing the physics equations and laws, chemical elements, historical years and facts, numbers and symbols, character sketches, personality traits, verses, speeches, vocabulary, etc., all sorts of data can be stored inside your memory palace. You just have to find an appropriate way to convert the data into manageable chunks and then store it.

For example, you cannot feed an entire 1000 words essay to the imaginary place. You have to extract key points in the introduction, body, and conclusion of the essay. By making small headings or symbolic phrases representing the subsequent information under that heading can compress the extended information in a comprehensive manner. This makes it easier to store the information in the locations present in the memory palace and visualize the information too.

* **Mnemonics**

The *mnemonics* are memory tools. Any method or learning technique that helps us to remember and retain the learned information is called a mnemonic device. The ancient Greek etymology of the word mnemonic suggests *memory* or *relating to memory.* By encoding the intended information in a specific way through imagery, symbols, acronyms, certain cues, hand gestures, infographics or lists, etc., the brain inputs the targeted information efficiently and quite symbolically. This increases the chances of successful retrieval of information at a later stage.

The success of mnemonics involves an underlying principle that the human mind gets more influenced by the symbolic data instead of abstract information.

A famous example of mnemonics can be the use of hands' knuckles to remember the number of days in a month.

The mnemonics technique was used in ancient history as well to help in remembrance of important data. This method evolved to be popularized as the *art of memory.* The significance of using the various techniques involving mnemonics made it an art unto itself. The principles of this art include *visualization, order, manageable data, association, effect, and repetition.* The *association principle* may involve the semantic priming method where the association between two words may enable memorization easily. That is where the concept of analogies came from. Grouping the relatable information into a single chunk makes it more logical for the brain to encode and remember. For example, remembering a phrase containing relatable words such as *a teacher and a student* is easier than the phrase *a teacher and a patient.*

The *effect principle* is quite an interesting aspect of the mnemonic technique. The fact that our brain encodes the information emotionally is understandable when we realize how a particular incident is remembered due to an element of surprise, pain or happiness attached to it. How often a particular memory is triggered by a similar emotion experienced in the present time. The *repetition principle* suggests the iterative philosophy of learning by constant revision.

Most of the following techniques listed below are the variants of the mnemonic method and are included in the arts of memory.

- **<u>Narrative Storytelling & Link Method</u>**

The human mind is interested in incidental happenings. A twist on an otherwise regular routine, a surprise element, a romanticized turn of events, and a dramatic affair. These factors make an interesting stimulation for the emotional brain. Memory can be served as a plot device in the story of your life. A climax or anti-climax related to incidental scenes in the storybook of which you are a character. When learning new things or memorizing several pieces of information together in a serialized manner, the storytelling method proves to be quite useful. The narration of events or things makes them more systematic and easier to remember. The linking of important events or objects by means of associating them with a narrative image makes them relatable and memorable.

For example, your toddler child has a collection of miscellaneous toys you want him to remember the names of, along with getting familiarized with the shape and functional purpose of each toy.

The list of targeted toys includes:

bed (miniature)

wallet

shopping basket

car

potted plant

broom

dustpan

glass

fence

Suppose you know about the link method and implement it by telling you child story by linking the toys together being narrated in a logical manner:

*"Hannah is a little girl. She loves plants. On a Sunday morning, she woke up early in the morning and her mother gave her a **glass** of milk as breakfast. Then her father told her that they would go shopping. She took the **shopping basket** from her mother. Her father and she sat in the **car**. They went to the local nursery to buy a **potted plant**. The nursery gate was surrounded by a white **fence**. The nursery was full of*

*trees, small plants, and grass. She saw a worker collecting dry leaves in a **dustpan** with the help of a **broom**. The gardener gave them the **potted plant**. Her father gave him the money from his wallet. Hannah carried the **potted plant** in the **shopping basket.** They returned home in the **car.** Hannah was very happy. She entered her mother's room. She saw her sitting on her **bed**. Hannah showed her the **potted plant** which they had bought. She liked it very much."*

The story can be demonstrated by the respective toy objects, appropriate facial expressions, and hand gestures. This way the names of objects and their usage can be engraved in the listening child's mind.

- **<u>Letter Patters</u>**

This strategy is not very common but can be effective in learning a specific text. Memorizing the lengthy text can be challenging, however, making use of letter patterns can make it easier. By making up a combination of short sentences describing the keynote of a portion of the text is what letter patterns do. Originally used for memorization of alphabetical letters formation in preschools, it has slowly become useful for adults as well. An example could be a description for a lengthy tutorial about computer processing:

"Input data as instruction, process information and display output by the control unit, store temporarily in RAM, optional permanent storage in the hard disk."

Another example could be of describing the shape formation to a beginner:

How an ellipse is formed?

"Make a horizontal line, make a vertical line in the middle to make a plus sign, join the ends of lines curvaceously."

This should be recited, following the actions to draw the shape in reality, making a lasting impression on the learner so that he can recall the catchphrase/mantra/ chant, etc., the next time he draws.

- ## **External Memory Devices**

You may have heard about the external memory of a computer. Flash drives, memory cards, hard disks, compact disks, etc., are all secondary/removable/ external devices for storage. Are you wondering why we are mentioning the computer's external devices here? Of course, to give you an example of how easily possible it is to leverage your memory instances by storing them in your journals, recording clips, thought wall, log files, etc. These are more like sources or tools instead of techniques for memory improvement but here we are mentioning it nevertheless because of the importance of this method to externalize your internal thoughts. Memories when externalized, become tangible pieces of important information that the brain feels consciously connected to. The conscious, repeated habit of making use of these tools to record past experiences, memory notes, and things to do, acts as a constant reminder to make the brain more active and present-minded even with respect to past events.

- ## <u>Mind or Concept Maps</u>

This technique is very productive to conceptualize the complex and detailed topics in a very comprehensive and concise manner. Often students are presented with concept maps at the beginning and end of a lesson to introduce and summarize the chapter respectively. The mapping of important information graphically makes it systematically classified in a logical way to understand and recall. For example, the following map represents the complex, full-length chapter about atomic structure:

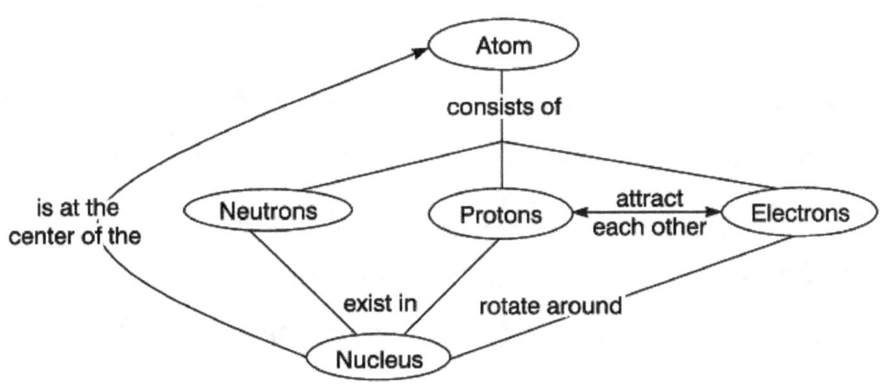

You can see how concise the data has become after being sketched out like this. The mind doesn't need to remember long definitions and textual explanations, yet it would still be able to describe the overall central idea, if an effectively displayed concept is used intelligently, like in mind mapping or concept mapping. Research shows the positive effects of this method in all sorts of ages, especially the youngsters as their analytical skills are sharper and could be used constructively here. Memory improvement training sessions involve the use of a textual explanation of an incident followed by a concept map blank template to be filled by the attendees. They can project their memories and thoughts into action on the map sheet, in order to revitalize their cognitive skills.

• **<u>Graphic Organizers</u>**

Graphical representation of information can be strikingly familiar and retainable for a long time in contrast to the textual one. There are numerous variants of graphic organizers used to depict the relational model between the combination of facts and ideas. Originally it is used as an umbrella term for all sorts of infographics and knowledge maps. However, as it is also called cognitive organizer, we will mention some subtle nuances that make a real difference.

Unlike other mind maps, mostly the graphical template blocks or flowcharts have question prompts to trigger the thought process. Creative thinking and reasoning skills can be enhanced exponentially using this technique. In reading comprehension, graphic organizers can be very constructive.

For instance, suppose you have read a particular novel in your English class and now you want to revise important details and memorize the plot well prior to attempting the exam. What you can do is, make out a template, organizing facts and outlining key questions like *What are the plot devices used in the opening chapter? Who are the most important characters? List down the physical traits of the protagonist. Summarize the anticlimactic scene at the end.*

Following graphic organizer template sourced from *dailyteachingtools.com* is an ideal example of usual graphic organizers used in high school classrooms for reading comprehension. The after-lesson practice of filling this organizer form can increase the memory retention of the learned concepts comprising the lesson or the novel previously taught in the class.

Characterization

Directions: There are four ways in which an author develops characters. Write one of your character's names in the center circle. Then, give an example of each characterization method in the appropriate outer circles.

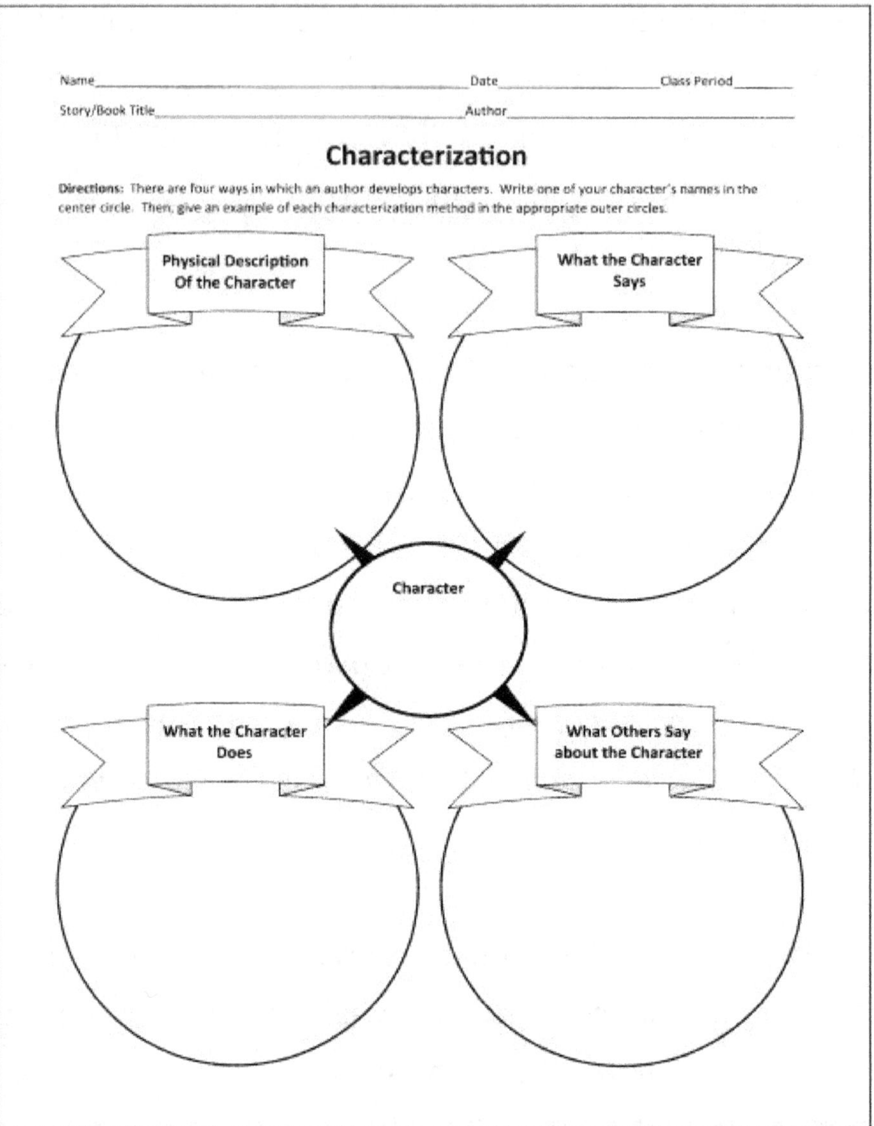

- **<u>Legend Lists</u>**

This technique is a self-improvised method for listing down pieces of data. The vertical lists are basically simple, linear stacking method for compiling the memory cabinet. The legend symbolism gives an opportunity to add meaningful tags in order to classify groups of similar tasks, objects, or facts. If you have a collection of miscellaneous tasks to be carried out or a list of diverse objects to be shopped from various locations. Try making a list of these assorted objects to be shopped for, using a specified legend system. Consider the example below:

- ☐ tea leaves
- ☐ cereals
- ☐ rice
- ☐ lentils
- ☐ coffee
- ☐ cake mix
- ☐ sugar
- ☐ juice
- ☐ salt
- ☐ medicine
- ☐ maple syrup

□ cottage cheese

At a glance, we can deduce that the above items are either liquids or solids. Allocate red (or any color of your choice) to liquids while blue (or any color of your choice) to solids. Make small colored squares in front of these items according to them belonging to either solids' group or liquids' group. Make a legend key at the top or bottom of the list in a prominent position depicting the color code.

- **Doodles / Graffiti**

If you have heard about a thought all before, hear it again in more detail here. Our mind's creative instincts once triggered, can keep generating ideas that swarm in mind making it abuzz. It needs an outlet to project them on a surface. If not given a chance for proper expression, it can cause frustration, over anticipation, and loss of focus resulting in hindered cognitive processes. The thought wall can be used not only for free self-expression but also to reinforce elemental ideas and previously learned facts. Enabling the expansive external display of one's internal thoughts can broaden the cognitive spectrum in a purposeful manner. Doodling or graffiti is an informal, candid recording or projection of ideas on the easily available surface. Mostly it serves as a therapeutic activity to release inner conflicts, memory struggles, and random; swarming notions in mind. In a way, it helps clean up the mind from trifling matters to let it regain lost focus. A person can also get a flashback of past instances of memory by reviewing his creative doodling on the idea-wall or in the memory journals.

- **<u>Chunking</u>**

The cognitive memory process can be accelerated by dividing information that is to be encoded, into chunks or individual data sets and then grouped together as larger sets. According to various researches made in cognitive psychology, it has been proven that chunking was the method of making productive use of working or short-term memory by means of holding few manageable chunks of information at a time. Chunking laid the foundation of several different memory concepts. The research also established the fact that a limited range of short-term memory to hold large pieces of data at a time causes people to be unable to retain information for long or memorize more things in a short time span.

Chunking involves the following basics:

- ✓ Know your mind by reviewing your prerequisite knowledge.
- ✓ Know the chunking principle; "Each skill or knowledge concept is made up of smaller chunks of interlinked concepts that are grouped in an integrated whole".
- ✓ As the capacity of your working memory is limited, mastering one small, individual chunk at a time makes you able to increase the range of both the short-term memory and the memorable information.
- ✓ The practiced, repeated chunking technique can make you capable of memorizing the smaller to the larger data set unconsciously. This way your memory will show considerable improvement.
- ✓ The chunking process can be subdivided into three main steps or phases:

- Searching the chunk-able information pattern in a given data group.
        - Breaking down the large data into smaller chunks and memorizing them.
        - Then using these smaller chunks in active practice.
    - The conscious phase is the first one where working memory focuses on analytical searching of the data to convert it into smaller chunks. After that, the process is almost an unconscious effort.

- **<u>Crosswords, puzzles, and Sudoku</u>**

Games such as crossword, hangman, anagram, puzzle, scrabble, chess, and Sudoku are quite a memory booster and external cognitive catalyst. They motivate the brain activity and accelerate the thinking skills. Experts believe that attempting a crossword activity on a daily basis can enhance memory. What happens is that your brain needs to think in all directions, combing through already known knowledge as well as opening sensory windows to accept newer, spontaneous ideas to solve these brain-teasing activities. It is a proven strategy that these brainers can help people with Alzheimer's too. People starting to show signs of memory decline should make some time for indulging in these games to give your brain some time for working out as these mini challenges can extend the mind power.

Scrabble, anagram, and hangman is a good choice for fun-filled brain exercise and memory recall or reconstruction. Especially these games can help in achieving high literacy and increases the power of speculation. Accelerating the numerical learning process through logical games like Sudoku also helps in unleashing that latent mental potential or energy that is said to store in our medulla oblongata or vertebral column.

Similarly, the jigsaw puzzles actually help in piecing together our random memories, converging them on a focal point that increases the mental concentration. When a missing piece gets fit in the puzzle, it makes our mind more driven towards a single goal, exercising it to the fullest. Several research studies show that as piecing together a jigsaw puzzle involves both the creativity and intuition of the right brain and logical reasoning of the left brain, this activity can stimulate the dual potential of the mind.

- **<u>Customized brain-teasing games (memory games)</u>**

Memory Game is a Montessori inspired innovative game to memorize numbers or words. It works on the principle of association, either by associating numbers with corresponding symbols or words with respective pictures or objects. It can be played in a group where a fixed number of people are present. There is a huge box having compartments equal to the number of people present. There are a couple of smaller boxes present in front of a group of people. One contains pictures of objects in the same number as the people present, while others contain the corresponding words' chits to be memorized.

- ✓ The conductor of the game, a memory trainer, will tell the members of the group that he will be telling them which picture to get.

- ✓ He will distribute the paper scraps or slips on which different words are written, one by one to each member.
- ✓ He will tell them not to show anyone their slip.
- ✓ Each group member will then be instructed to go and take out the picture corresponding to the word written on their slip, from the box and put it inside their compartment in the larger box.
- ✓ The instructor will ask everyone to carefully look and guess which word the person got.
- ✓ Then each person will do the same for their paper slip.

This game can be an interesting grouped exercise for recalling the previously learned vocabulary. It is a twofold revision technique as the person associating the word with the picture is testing his own memory, while others who don't know which word he got, are testing their own memories by guessing as they watch him take out the corresponding picture and put it inside his compartment in the larger box.

- ### **First and last letter association with link method**

Almost similar to acronyms (another mnemonic strategy) with a subtle difference that acronyms are pronounceable, word- letter association is an intelligent technique of memorizing quickly by making logical associations with the first or last letter of a word. By fixating a significant word as a full form for each word of a long sentence can make it quite easy to learn and remember. For example,

Great minds think alike is an idiomatic phrase, if you want to memorize it quickly you may review that it can associatively be distributed to become:

"G M T A"

Similarly, the last letter association technique where the last letter of a word could be associated with a concept or image to help remember a related thought.

The link method in the same context can help you to memorize things better still. For example, if you want to remember the sentence:

"The computer is a processing device."

Write each word in a vertical column separately, as individual units. See this sequence:

The

Computer

Processes

Information

Now, take each word's initial letter to write together like this:

TCPI

When you later need to remember this sentence, you simply have to recall this combination of initial letters. This technique also helps in taking a snapshot of the available information in such visual prominence that the mind can clearly retrieve the intended information due to the flashes of these snapshots at the time of recall.

- **<u>Alphanumerical Associative Combinations</u>**

Sometimes, to enhance the memory efficiency to recall numbers systems and numeric sequences. Each chunk of numbers contains a limited number of numeric symbols that can be associated with alphabets or words. Many aptitude tests and analytical reasoning exercises involve this technique to decode or decrypt information. For example, to memorize the number set:

2 3 4 1 5 3 6 2

Associate with each number, its corresponding alphabet in the sequence of its place of order. Such as 1 represents A, 2 represents B, and so on.

- **<u>Treasure Hunt for Words or Objects</u>**

Muscular memory is a type of memory that helps familiarize the muscles of the body with a particular environment, structure, or place by means of exploring it with the tactile sense (sense of touch), often done with closed eyes, it can be done with opened eyes as well. While playing a treasure hunt, sensory reception is sharpened due to touch and search. The treasure hunt for words can be an interesting stimulator for a curious search for information not only physically but mentally too. Objects to be memorized are hidden inside certain places in a room preferably with shelves. Each hidden object is searched by following a trail of innovative cues found in various nooks and corners. A person searching, if follows the clues accordingly, will be ultimately led to the hidden object, triggering his analytical and memory skills along the way.

- **<u>Spotlight Method</u>**

This famous method is a proven strategical method for memorizing information in flashes. The spot-light or flashbulb uses a beam of focused light projected on a particular area of information (for e.g. selected textual paragraph). The room should be in complete darkness while the only light emitting from the spot-bulb or flashlight illuminates the selected information to be memorized. This method helps the brain to encode the text as images that can deeply be implanted in the brain through the retina. This is also called the military method due to its resemblance to some of the similar techniques used by them. The flashlight can be turned on and off more than a couple of times to repeatedly imprint the textual image in mind. The technique can be applied for memorization of maps, pictures, graphs, etc., as well.

- **<u>Color Coding</u>**

The color coding is a popular trend to set up an organized system in any particular environment. Be it the arrangement of spices in the kitchen, orderly display of clothes and shoes in the dressing room, or the classification of jewelry in your vanity closet. The objects when coded in a pre-determined format based on a color legend, can be easily retrievable. For e.g. blue studs and pendant along with other blue trinkets are put in a blue-colored box, red in red, yellow in yellow and so on. Some objects if not colored can still be color-coded by customization. For e.g. in your filing cabinet, all the files that you have are brown in color. You can place a color identifier or legend on the spines of the file on the region where it can be shown as soon as the cabinet is opened to retrieve any file. Draw a legend key describing each color code, with a respective group of files and topics, on the cabinet door to refer to it each time you need to search a particular group. When this orderly format is followed, it brings peace of mind and internal satisfaction is achieved due to the avoidance of chaos.

- **<u>Group Discussions, Memory Portals or Forums, and Blogging</u>**

Humans tend to open newer doors of knowledge and learning through interaction and socialization. Brainstorming ideas, revising old concepts, and sharing past experiences can bring considerable improvement in mind power and idea restoration or generation.

- **<u>Songs, Parodies, & Poems</u>**

This particular technique is an absolute favorite of many people having a creative mind and humorous disposition. Learning recipes, authors' names, historical events, chemical elements, significant dates and years, main essay headings, idioms, etc., all sorts of information can be memorized by verification technique. You just need to put the concepts into a rhyme or poem format or making an informative yet humorous parody of an already famous song, all this

so that you can revise and recall things effortlessly.,
For e.g., you need to memorize the function of pineal
gland in neuroscience,

You can make a parody of famous children's poem and
incorporate the intended concept in it to make the
memorization easier:

(Parody of twinkle twinkle, little star)

Pineal, pineal, little gland you are,
your other tasks are still bizarre,
though you bring some sleep to the eye,
secreting melatonin when night stops by!

The following picture shows another rhyming memory
technique called pegging system:

Visual Mnemonics: Peg-word system

- Technique used to memorise lists of words

- Learn basic organisational structure......

One is a bun
Two is a shoe
Three is a tree
Four is a door
Five is a hive
Six are sticks
Seven is heaven
Eight is a gate
Nine is a line
Ten is a hen

- **<u>Willpower & Conscious Effort</u>**

Though familiar incidents, memory devices like patterns and pegging, visual linkages, and other environmental stimuli do activate the memory and accelerate the learning process, it can still be less effective if not accompanied by a constant inner will to achieve improvement. As mentioned earlier, the increase in confidence level can consequently increase the brainpower improvement levels. Humans are a wonderful creation of God. They have the potential to achieve amazing things if they put their mind to it. As the old saying goes, determination breeds success, you can improvise a little and update it a little according to the *mind over matter principle:*

"Man breeds determination in his mind, which materializes as success in his life."

Your vigor of mind and mental thought process will determine your strength of the memory. There is an optimistic thought, even if you think you may have a below-average memory, realize that you do tend to know and try to remember what's important to you. At the end of the day, cling to this positive notion and improve your memory by practicing these techniques.

Chapter5: What is a Photographic Memory?

Also sometimes referred to as Eidetic memory, the photographic memory is an enabling capacity of the brain to recall images, text, graphical symbols, etc. with shocking clarity after being exposed to them for a short span of time, in some cases only seconds or instances.

Generally, it is seen that people are more inclined towards visual patterns and can memorize them easily. However, the people with eidetic memory can literally take a snapshot of the information and save them exactly as it is in their mind without having to use any sort of specific mnemonic or memory improvement technique. Sounds great, doesn't it?

Imagine yourself carrying a natural medium-sized camera in place of your head and another tiny one in place of your eyes, all the information in the world could be captured in the blink of an eye and within a passing impulse inside the mind. How wonderful is that! All the memories could become a scrapbook or photo album in your head, stored in the respective compartments. Whenever a particular memory is needed to be accessed, you could just skim through the album to retrieve the particular photo. However, here comes the catch, not everyone is born with a naturally gifted Eidetic or photographic memory.

Photographic Memory in Early Years

Research shows that it is rare to witness a truly eidetic memory in adults, however, in early years children often go through a phase where they tend to develop a sort of memory which enables them to observe objects for a short span of time and recall them afterward in vivid detail. This mostly happens when a child is exploring his environment, his young mind is like an absorbing sponge, taking in all the impressions and exposed details of the surroundings and memorizing them exactly as they are. There are also several sensitive periods of development at work in the early years. Children accumulate all the available knowledge consciously or unconsciously and language acquisition also occurs at that time.

Educationists suggest that the symbols or flashcards used in preschool setups are actually a tool to enhance the child's photographic memory and make use of his visual sense in order to speed up the learning and memorization of sight words and sounds. Similarly, many activities in the early years' classroom are planned to facilitate learning through visual charts and pictures.

Sometimes children are even asked to touch the objects and feel them in order to remember the shape and recall it later. Many irregular words that cannot be read phonetically i.e. sound by sound are often listed under puzzle words and are taught to the child as a visual image. In this way, the child's photographic memory is triggered and he is able to memorize them with ease. The word becomes a complete picture in front of his eyes and he quickly saves it in his mind without having to break the word into sound letters to read it. Statistics show that after growing up, many adults who had a good photographic memory at some stage in their childhood, tend to find difficulty in memorizing things. So, what is the mystery behind photographic memory? Can it be acquired at a later stage in life? Can it be lost forever or strengthened further with practice? Let's explore these inevitable questions below.

Photographic Memory in Adults

Brain experts claim that what we generally see nowadays is only a small part of what a photographic memory could really be. Some adults may be able to distinctly remember the images or text that they saw only for a few seconds, however, a completely advance photographic memory may not exist in our world as there is no actual evidence seen to date, of someone possessing it in its entirety. What we can do though is, practice some strategies to acquire something close to it. A strong memory that can help us remember things vividly. To be honest, we actually don't need a photographic memory as it can be chaotic at times.

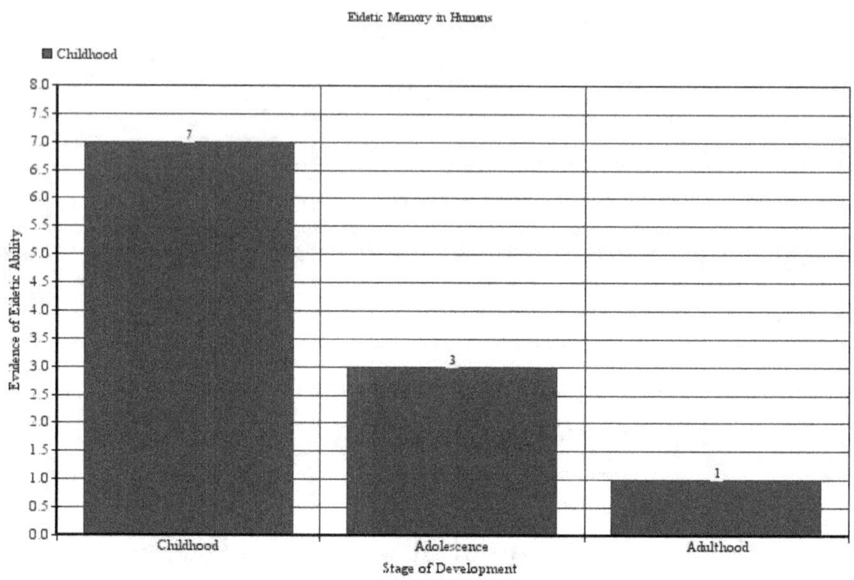

Cognitive psychologists agree that if an adult person was to have a photographic memory, due to his vast exposure, socialization, numerous daily experiences, he would have stored so many memories in his mind that even recalling them would become a chore, albeit organizing them. As compared to an adult, a child is more likely to be happy with a photographic memory. His limited experiences and exposure would enable him to store the information with clarity and recall them instantly too without having to go through thousands of stored virtual images every now and then. Instead, concentration is the key as our goal is not to distract our mind due to irrelevant images, but making it focus more on the task at hand.

Actionable Tips to Memorize Photographically

There was a game we used to play as a kid. One of us would place a series of objects upon a desk in a particular sequence. Then he would ask us to glance at the desk momentarily to perceive the displayed setting before closing our eyes. Now he will ask us one by one, what did we see on the desk. Everyone would try to describe in great detail, all the objects that they saw along with a description of the order in which they were placed. The description would, of course, be according to their perception and observation. Here the individual power of our memory would become evident. If we miss out on the details, the points will get deducted from our scorecard. Similarly, if someone would succeed in getting all the details correct, they would get to win the *"brilliant picture memory"* badge. Recalling and replaying this game, we can relive those experiences and revitalize our memories.

So, are you ready to learn those 10 universally actionable tips that we have hand-picked for you to be practiced along with different memory improvement techniques? These tips are like maxims that lay a foundation for improved memory. Once the ground is laid and a mechanism forms, you can start seeing the results soon.

1. Observation:

This is an incredible tool to master the art of knowledge acquisition. Observation is basically a gateway to learning new things. A sort of microscope through which even the minutest details can be recorded. Those who practice the art of observation are often the ones who successfully improve their memory power in the long run. Things are always angular. Every other glance at them will reveal a newer angle to the keen eye. A good observer not only observes the details but absorbs it too.

This trait can be very helpful in developing the ability to memorize things photographically.

How would you find that you can become a good observer? It's simple. First, try to check if you have got those telling signs in you. Do you often tend to look around while waiting for a flight in a departure lounge? Are you keen to stand in the balcony and glance at the passerby when you have nothing else to do? Do you often find yourself as part of an audience rather than on stage, in action? Be rest assured, you have got it in you. You can do this!

The AFDOC principle of observation and its elements:

- Be Attentive:

One of the most important open secrets of a good observation is the ability to pay attention to the slightest of details. You can never be too attentive when it comes to observing a scenario. When practicing the drill, you will get to know how often we miss the most obvious details due to a lack of proper attention. Haven't you encountered at times, the trouble of forgetting the easiest things in daily life? Yes, it sucks but it can be cured. Keep reading to find out.

- Be Determined:

This is actually the driving force behind every success story. Determination, stemming from a constant need to prove yourself and succeed. A sizeable bout of determination can push you in the right direction. As an observer, you have to persevere and collect the information keenly. Don't give up, practice daily. It is not a one-time deal. It is a continuous process of making the brain get used to the idea of clear-headed perception and detailed observation.

- Be Hasty:

Yes, you read it right. Careful haste is something that you have to develop in order to absorb every detail in a given timeframe. Being slow and lazy will not work for you here. By being quick, you will stimulate your brain to accelerate the functional processes of perception, hearing, and listening, etc. This way you will gain speed and push your potential to the optimum. Several of the unused connections of the brain can be alternatively used to speed up the processes, hence fueling the neurotransmitters and oiling the pathways that were corroded due to lack of use.

- Be Objective:

Being accurate, unbiased, and objective is the key to an honest observation. Always remember to feed a perfect memory to your brain, the original incident should be clear and accurate. Or else the memory would be hazy as the facts become jumbled up with your own opinions and overshadowed by your personal judgments. Until when the time comes to recall it, you would be confused by the very fact that whether what you recall actually happened or at least a part of it is only a figment of your imagination.

- Be Curious:

Remember that the person not *willing* to learn new things can *never* learn. Remember that the person not *interested* in improving his memory can *never* improve it. If you are observing something, try to take a deliberate interest in it. Try to be curious about the details that are visible. Try to explore the possible angles that are not so obvious at first glance but can become apparent at a second or third glance. Curiosity may have killed the cat, but here the case is quite different. Lack of curiosity may kill your interest and willingness to learn and memorize, hence killing the chances of improvement.

2. Concentration:

Concentration not only makes a person focused but also levelheaded. Once you decide to converge your energies on a targeted focal point, you can even burn the lens if you want i.e. hitting the target successfully. Never set yourself aboard an unrealistic goal. Trying to practice all sorts of techniques and memorizing numerous things simultaneously can diverge your energies until they burn out, instead of converging them on a common goal point.

The brain hangs up and tends to shut down like an exhausted computer if instructed to perform a multitude of heavy tasks at a time. All of us have experienced a load of learning material to revise prior to the exam. How much the mind diverts while memorizing a particular topic when a pile of other topics is beside you, begging to be revised. Naturally, you have to prioritize and organize in order to avoid losing your concentration.

Just like that, if you don't select a setting to be observed priorly, you may glance at other things during the observation outside your selected frame which may result in lost focus, missed details and an overall decline in the level of concentration. Memorizing photographically needs you to concentrate on the task at hand. Stop being distracted by random thoughts. They say that thinking meaningfully is the only way to think because thinking without meaning or purpose is basically overthinking which is quite exhaustive in nature and detrimental to your memory. When so many thoughts are accumulated in the brain, the old gold ones become older and are get buried under random pebbles. Digging becomes a cumbersome task and they become long forgotten, while the mind becomes full of meaningless trash.

3. Order:

Order is a word which itself is very orderly. Just look at how it smoothly rolls off the tongue when articulated. Precise and collected, it should be inculcated in your daily memory drills. As the mind senses order, it becomes calm. This way it is able to collect and recollect incidents and experiences clearly. Bring order in your study notes, kitchen cabinets, workspace, clothing closets, nightstand, and even your bric-a-brac section. You would have heard about people being able to walk in the dark inside their homes, correctly guessing the place of things, position of furniture, and direction of rooms. Some of them even know a particular room should be a certain number of steps farther from their standing point. They can even discover a particular object they are searching for from a drawer of a dressing table or vanity cabinet. All of this is possible because they have arranged things in their life in an orderly manner. You can do that too.

This will not only improve your memory greatly but also enable your brain to function in a systematic manner. On the other hand, chaos will only bring disturbing thoughts and feelings which can damage the brain's will to encode new information or retrieve the older one.

4. Confidence:

Confidence is not just a word, it is an entire system of beliefs. Believing in your ability to move forth. Believing in your need to improve. Believing in your strengths and positive traits. Believing in your determination to succeed. Most importantly,

"believing in your memories."

This may sound strange, but you have to be confident not only at the time of storing the information but also at the time of retrieving it. You are sure that you have memorized something yet you lose confidence in your ability to recall it. How can that be a successful mindset? The brain needs assurance. You provide it with your words when you give your brain a pep talk, and with your actions too, when you are learning new things with a determination to recall it afterward.

5. Clarity:

This is part and parcel of focus and concentration. Even if you have preselected your subject of memorization and are singularly pursuing it, you may encode the intended information along with a lot of fluctuations. Try to clear out those pathways to receive a clear message. A blurred message is encoded when some sort of residual stress or disturbing thoughts are lurking behind the scenes. Make sure you are not falling prey to these grainy thoughts that spoil the whole clarity of a message, thus storing a shady memory.

6. Positivity:

Making yourself influenced by your dark experiences may preoccupy your mind, thus stopping your ability to make room for newer memories. A negative mindset even subdues your zest for regaining mind power or building it anew. Stop dwelling on that one incident where you flunked an exam or lost in a spelling bee contest. Mind you, memories can be rewritten so it can be the past. History may repeat itself, but the repeating pattern is decided by the people themselves. If you have lost in the past, the loss may reoccur but maybe not for you this time. Believe it! Being positive is the way towards accumulating all the right information in your mind. The one which is easily retained and recalled as it is something you want to hold on to. It is something you *want* to happen *again* and *again.* Your mind remembers that it is important to you, healthy for you, thus it cooperates.

7. Compartmentalization:

Now, this is something easier done than said. As the word suggests, this is a method of actionable sorting and management of the brain's junk. Consider your mind as a large walk-in closet. Each set of accessories has a dedicated space allocated for it. The clothes go in the hangers inside the wardrobe space on the right-hand side. The shoes displayed nicely on the left side shoe rack. The jewelry tucked in safely inside a gorgeous vanity case set upon the dressing table, across the frontal wall. The rule of thumb is:

" A thing for a place and a place for a thing."

Suppose, you enter the closet, walk through it, you are in a hurry to get ready for work. You grab the wardrobe door, slide it quickly to reveal an array of clothes hanging. Every other set of clothes beckons to you. You rummage through them in a haphazard way, grabbing a few, replacing them again, looking for a particular piece then compromising on another due to lack of time. You quickly change leaving a mismanaged mess in your wake, reassuring yourself you will see to it *later*.

Moving towards the dressing table, you pick up a brush, yank through your hair, a couple of things may fall from the table in your haste to search for a bottle of moisturizer or a particular mist or that perfect pair of earrings. Then comes the turn for shoes, each pair is placed in order but for some unknown reason, you can't find those regular black pumps. You hunt through the shoe rack and at the last minute find them actually sitting on the very top shelf, quite obvious to the calm eye.

While you put them on, you send a cursory glance to the resulted state of your shoe rack, after what you did in your quest to find the most obvious thing. You push the depressing thought of this messy state of affairs aside, and vow to deal with it *later.* We all know that *later,* soon becomes history.

This sort of sorry story happens inside our brain too. The orderly nature of the brain by default compels it to install each memory in a particular section. Making it organized and easy to retrieve. But when chaos occurs in your life and you are short on schedule, you ransack your brain, hurriedly rummaging through the compartments or sections in search of a particular memory. This random marauding makes it nearly impossible for your brain to keep compartmentalizing things. What you can do to avoid this is, associate each memory with a particular incident or scenario. Link together similar sorts of experiences in an array or chain of memories that can be triggered one after the other by a particular picture, journal entry, color, or catchphrase, or word.

Here we can consider the case of a middle-aged housewife named Sarah. She wants to keep order in her life and maintain her memories and brain activity in an organized manner. By jotting down her notes, recipes and pantry lists in her cooking journal, she maintains a record of her kitchen experiences. She also adds time and again, snapshots of specific moments that she wants to remember. A picture of a perfectly cooked meal perhaps, or an ideal sequence of utensils in the cabinet, or maybe a perfect combination of ingredients for a spur of a moment personally customized recipe. These things keep her kitchen department and its respective mind compartment in order. Now, whenever she needs to remember a certain recipe, she may just flip through a set of pictures depicting the ingredients and all the necessary procedures and relevant steps are recalled in a flash. Similarly, she compartmentalizes her socialization and family gatherings. A particular sitting arrangement and hospitality method for a particular guest can help her recall the previous meeting with the same person. She maintains a meeting log, making sections dedicated to her most frequent guests and social meetings. Through regular log entries such as concise phrases, socio-grams, or a clicked photo to commemorate the event, she can be more spontaneous in her responses while socializing. For her, every passing day becomes as easy to remember as the present day. People often get surprised and popular comments are;

"Sarah has a very good memory, she even remembers what dress Anna's baby girl wore at the previous annual community dinner"
or
"Sarah always remembers to serve me her delicious coffee in that large black ceramic mug that I love so much"
or
"Sarah is a lady of honor, she remembered what she promised me even after so much time has passed".

The above case shows that compartmentalizing your memories is an effective way to increase your power to retain or retrieve them. To a very busy person, Sarah may seem to have so much extra time at hand to invest in journaling and logging all the time. But the truth is, Not doing so will waste your time more in the long run.

Systematic conditioning of the brain is very important to avoid future disruption.

Moreover, once you get the hang of things you master the speed and accuracy at the same time i.e. you may not need to spend as much time on these trivial records in the future as your brain will get used to picking up the important details, distributing them into respective compartments. It will develop an affinity with storing what is needed, discarding what is not, retaining what is always needed, recalling what is occasionally needed.

8. Repetition:

Can you teach a goat something, anything?

Maybe yes, but can you teach it to recite a poem instead of uttering *baa* each time it opens its mouth?

Maybe not! But if *you* want to memorize something like a poem may be, you can by teaching a goat. No kidding. People repeat things in front of their pets as though they are teaching them, talking to them, regardless of what their response is. This constant repetition helps them memorize the subject fast. People are seen repeating and practicing in front of a mirror prior to making a public speech, etc.

Why do they do so?

Because, perhaps the very idea of just facing yourself without interruption or unnecessary criticism appeals to them, calm their nerves don, boost their confidence further. In the case of repeating and memorizing a poem in front of a pet, perhaps the innocence of a pet appears less intimidating, so they can focus more on the words they are reciting without stressful distraction.

All in all, the idea of repetition is the crux of memorization. The connections in the brain are improved and strengthened when similar actions are repeated again and again until the brain gets so familiar with certain functions, you can even recall them in sleep. You can recall where you left off a conversation even after hours have passed, you would even be able to utter a sentence in the same tone of voice and with the same gesture and facial expression. That is often seen when people have watched a particular theatrical performance or comedy show multiple times repeatedly, they can mimic the expressions exactly as they saw. If you want to improve your memory to a nearly photographic level, repetition and revision is a mandatory practice.

9. Implementation:

Several of us have heard the famous hierarchy of educational learning called *the bloom's taxonomy.* It has three domains essentially i.e. cognitive, affective or emotional, psychomotor (relating to the mind and body). The cognitive domain is mostly used in the academic sense. It has six levels or steps that can be implemented in a sequence to ensure effective learning outcomes. These six levels are placed in the pyramid hierarchical model and comprise (from bottom to top): *knowledge, comprehension, application, analysis, evaluation, and synthesis.* Many universities and colleges and even secondary schools follow this model to devise lesson plans, assessments, and research activities. The *application* stage is basically the implementation.

Consider a student Ben, today he has been introduced to a new science topic about light and electricity in his class.

The teacher has stated and defined the term electricity and then ask the students to repeat what they learned. Level 1, i.e. knowledge has been achieved. But this is only the start. Ben's brain has gained information and stored it but is he able to understand or comprehend the concept of how light or electricity works? This remains open for discussion.

The next day, his teacher makes him sit in a study group with his peers to *discuss* and *explain* what they understood by the previous day's definition. Ben is able to *recall* some of the words, maybe, but the concept is not that clear. After discussion though, they may be able to explain a little in their own words. Level 2 i.e. *comprehension* would be accomplished after further explanation of the concept by the teacher and the ability of the students to *summarize* that explanation in their own words.

The third stage starts when the teacher assigns a project to the students to make a simple circuit or a toy torch to *apply* their *knowledge* and *comprehension* practice. This gives them the chance to implement the learned concepts and the knowledge is retained as the memory improves with repetition and implementation of the same concepts over and over again. This is not where the learning ends though, the higher stages in this taxonomy suggest more abstract thinking and practices that can be glimpsed in the following figure depicting Bloom's cognitive model in great detail:

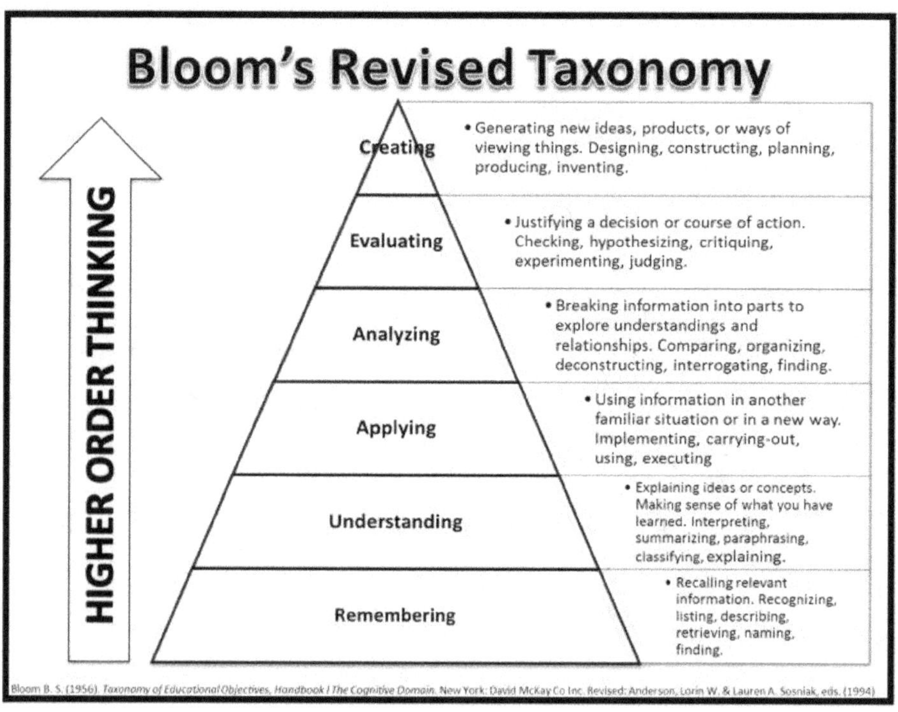

In 1956's older version of the bloom's taxonomy placed *synthesis* before the *evaluation* stage. Which puts the concept of assessment or examination of facts and knowledge to create or synthesize newer strategies or ideas, in a wrong sequence. The modernized version came after results gathered from the academic statistics and students' and teachers' experiences. The altered version placed the *evaluation* or assessment stage before the *synthesis.* Therefore, it has been proven that knowledge after it is gained, is retained by understanding, repetition, implementation, evaluation or examination, and finally creating or synthesizing a new whole by putting together miscellaneous parts of previous knowledge. That's how inventions happen in our world!

10. Assessment:

This tip is a nail in the coffin. You lock your important memory by assessing it through various practice tests, quizzes, and questionnaires. You test your brain and condition it to be capable of conjuring the required information with detail the instant you summon it. Why the exams are so important? Why every academic institute create such a hype over admission tests, aptitude exams, and classroom assessments? Because this is the easiest way for them to check if you actually remember what you have learned previously. In order to not waste their time or yours, they need to be sure that knowledge is being invested, not wasted.

The brain's rule of thumb or knowledge is, *use it or lose it.* like it or not, it works that way. Your brain has a knack of discarding garbage and it is always on an automated mode when it comes to dumping waste. The brain's standard for measuring whether a particular piece of memory or information is important or not is to check how frequently it is recalled and how *useful* and *used* it is.

Chapter6: Cramming v/s Spacing v/s Accelerated Learning

Imagine going for a vacation. last-minute packing is remaining. Travel bags are all full to the neck. No space for a couple of extra clothes, that comfy green jumper, or a pair of newly bought sneakers. What do you often do? Tie the sweater around the strap or wear the sneakers yourself instead? or maybe opening the zip wide, pushing the clothes that are already inside, even more inside with a fist, to make a nonexistent space for some last-minute add-ins. This is what cramming is!

Have you tried a napkin dance before? Contesting couples are given a piece of napkin each and are told to dance standing on their respective napkin without stepping outside of the limited space. After every music break, the napkin is folded once. In the first round, the napkin is a single-layered square, then a two-layered rectangle, then 4 layered square again, until the time comes when most of the couples are eliminated due to stepping outside the narrow and congested surface inevitably. This is what cramming is!

Cramming

In a strictly academic sense, students cram when they tend to take in too much information in too little a time. They revise large piles of books in a single night before a particular exam, crowding their brain in the process. This sort of cramming largely happens when students procrastinate the entire academic year, don't set their priorities straight, and don't allocate appropriate hours for both study and play. The misbalance in sleep, play, socialization, and studies results in a compulsive need to cram every book before an exam, burning the midnight oil.

Most students claim that they have aced an exam while preparing only a night before. But if you closely enquire, you will come to know that most of those who actually achieved good grades even after only a night of revision are the ones who paid attention in the class throughout the year or at least attended most of the lectures. If that is not the case then they dedicated some portion of their time to self-studying and covering the missed topics. However, the results are not often satisfactory due to mental stress, lack of sleep, and sluggish brain activity. Think of it as a traffic jam when roads are crammed with vehicles of all sort, honking from every direction, trying to grab attention. It is a nightmare in making or a disaster waiting to happen.

The study is not magic, it is a habit. You work hard, you learn, you revise, you succeed. It is simple. For some of you, the requirement level of hard work may vary but still, it is required by all. A student who doesn't appear to note down anything during a lecture about the national economy may have absorbed it word by word through attentive listening skills. He may even be discussing the same topic with his peers outside the class context, explaining it, again and again, giving reference to it in daily conversations at home during evening tea, relating it to the real-world examples during shopping for groceries in a supermarket. Whereas a student who has scribbled throughout the lecture, making important notes in his journal, may not even open it at home afterward albeit discussing or revising it until the very night before the exam. Who, do you think is likely to succeed more in the exam or at least has developed a better level of understanding which is the main aim of studying? Who do you think will be able to readily recall the concepts that were explained in the class, even if not the exact words of the lecture? Of course, the one who has maintained a close connection with the learned concepts in any form throughout the year instead of one who succumbed to cramming as a last resort.

Spacing

Many of us have, consciously or unconsciously, tried a method of revision where you are asked a set of questions by your partner. Whenever you fail to answer a particular one, your partner tells the correct answer and then moves towards the next ones, only to come back later to ask the missed question again. This time you may answer it correctly.

Spaced learning was first introduced by Hermann Ebbinghaus, a psychologist and memory researcher belonging to Germany. He got his inspiration from the work of Gustav Fechner, also a psychologist who wrote a book about his experimental findings on psychophysics. As mentioned above, Ebbinghaus was quite passionate in his quest for examining the mysterious workings of mind and memory. It was this persistence in experimenting everything personally without getting overshadowed by prevalent theories, which led him to discover his famous forgetting curve. You read about memory loss in chapter no. 2. However, here we will relate it with the spaced learning effect.

So, let us first understand what spaced learning really is?

Spaced learning or spacing technique is the method of distributing information over an extended period of time, inserting short intervals of distraction in between. This method is proven to be far more effective than cramming where you try to accumulate a large volume of knowledge in a very short time span. Spaced learning is more systematic and result oriented. Rather than stretching it in a single session, why not spread it over multiple sessions?

Remember,

Stretching brings strain and tension while spreading brings richness in approach and flexibility.

Equally effective in both formal and informal learning contexts, and for both children and adults, people can efficiently learn skills such as vocabulary, numbers, art techniques, culinary skills, etc. by spacing the content that is to be learned and memorized. Even the classroom blocks or periods in a school are scheduled in such a way that learning is mostly preceded by an assembly or physical exercise and proceeded by a game unit or recess. This helps students to release their pent-up frustrations and get distracted in a good way, refreshing them to start memorizing them anew. It also eliminates the possibility of getting the knowledge that was acquired in the previous session mixed up with the one acquired in the next session. So here comes the compartmentalizing. Each session's information is tucked away safely, labeled and locked, not to be confused with another topic. Thus the order prevails and the performance improves. Next time you sit for a revision, make sure you set a realistic timeframe and divide the selected content into manageable portions spread across that timeframe with recreational breaks in between. You will understand the art of spaced learning and experience its perks first hand.

How do we forget and remember?

Ebbinghaus observed that the mind can dispose of the unused information with the passage of time. The hypothesis he proposed after his observations and experiments became the beginning of forgetting theory. According to the results of his memory testing over a period of time, he plotted a graph that materialized as a curve showing the diminishing memory as time passes. This curve is called the *forgetting curve*. If it wasn't the case of us forgetting things, no one had to revise anything. The concept of repetition wouldn't have existed. The memory loss and its nature can be defined by the forgetting curve.

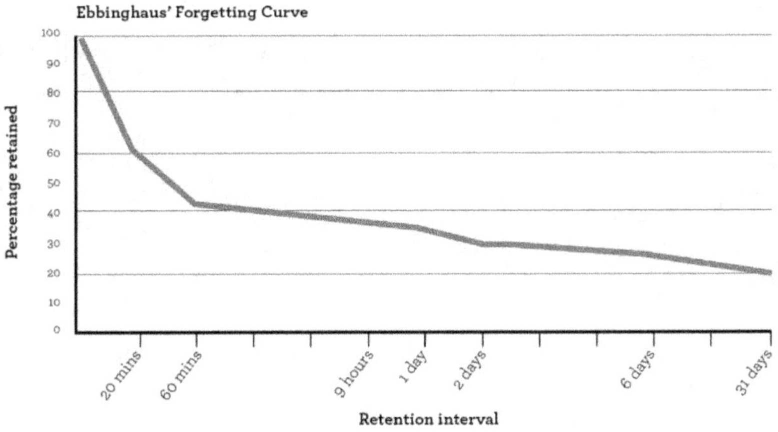

Why do we forget and remember

Why crammed facts soon disappear from the mind is because the curve shows us that information recently acquired is the fastest to lose. The exponential drop occurs within minutes of learning a thing if not given frequent, timely reminders day after day. It is where the role of spaced repetition comes in. The *forgetting curve* can be changed into a *learning curve* or slope by way of spaced memorization technique, also called distributed learning. To slow down the forgetting process, you need to provide your recent memory some robustness and longevity by revisions and repetition over time. Because the content of large length can simply not be memorized in single repetition without enough reminders; no matter how much the concentration or attention is paid. Even the small piece of content needs a couple of revisions to be able to recall exactly.

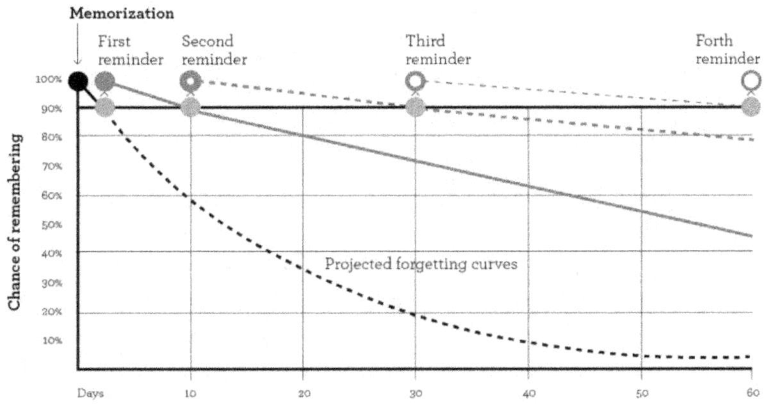

What do we forget and remember

We, humans, are emotional beings to the extreme. We breathe emotions, talk emotions, and feel emotions. We even think emotionally. We cannot separate the emotions and intensity of some level from our thoughts and responses. What we remember is most of the time attached to our hearts. Some incident that has an emotional story behind it. Some intense moments of self-realization, success, or disappointment. We cannot help stereotyping our memories by labeling them as happy, sad, or hilarious. We even train our brain to be nostalgic about a past incident and thus our brain becomes emotional too. If that is how we tend to function most of the time, why not take it to our advantage?

The intensity of the things experienced the first time, help us recall them the second time we feel the same intensity while experiencing other things. We attempt to correlate the experiences of a similar intensity that aroused a similar emotion in us. when something seems worth remembering, just mark it as important and your brain would *feel* the urgency of emotion and its importance. In his text, *"Memory and Forgetting"*, Ebbinghaus described the importance of attention, interest, intensity, and concentration for the retention of memory. Even to be able to reproduce the experiences and tasks, there should be some greater level of intensity of interest attached. Interest or focus alone, while observing someone will not suffice. A shocking incident has an element of surprise in it and is likely to be remembered more than an ordinary one that occurs almost daily.

Suppose, you visit a park daily, you encounter many passersby, you cannot remember all of them. But this morning when you passed the walking track you saw a boy wearing a neon orange jumper suit, yelling at the top of his lungs, chasing after a runaway dog. You were startled for a second due to his screaming. You are likely to remember him or a while may be due to his unusual suit color or his unusual behavior or his runaway pet that gave a bit of a shock. And when you recall the incident, you may also experience the same emotion associated with it.

Accelerated Learning

They say relearning is better than learning and recall is better than identification. It is true. Why are you advised to practice mock tests and quizzes rather than linearly reading through the book? Because most important is to *recall* and *retrieve* your previously learned knowledge. These revision tests are specifically designed to trigger the diminishing memory and highlight the key points enabling you to get a grip on nearly lost information.

This is one of the reasons why a highlighter should always be in your hand while listening to a lecture or reading through a text during self-study. Highlighting the most important details and description during your study will help you at the time of revision. You can just review the highlighted part of the paragraph to be able to remember what was discussed in the whole paragraph. This way you can not only save time but also increase performance and accelerate the overall learning and relearning process. This, in fact, is one of the several techniques of accelerated learning.

Accelerated learning can be defined as the process of interactive learning that is learner-centered and provides room for learners taking the initiative. It is an activity-based, stimulating method that urges the learner to be involved in the learning process as a whole. Shunning the passive, prolonged methods of conventional teaching, an accelerated learning educator adapts the role of a facilitator rather than an instructor enhancing the cognitive potential of the learner to the optimum. Through various activities, the learner is given a chance to explore and discover things through actively exercising his creativity, memory power, and previous experiential knowledge. He can implement ideas and make meaningful creations that take him from known to the unknown. The idea of scaffolding and Zone of Proximal Development (ZPD) is taken to the next level here. ZPD suggests an area that ranges between what a learner can do on his own, what he would be able to do if provided some assistance (this assistance or guidance is called *scaffolding*), and what he has yet to achieve.

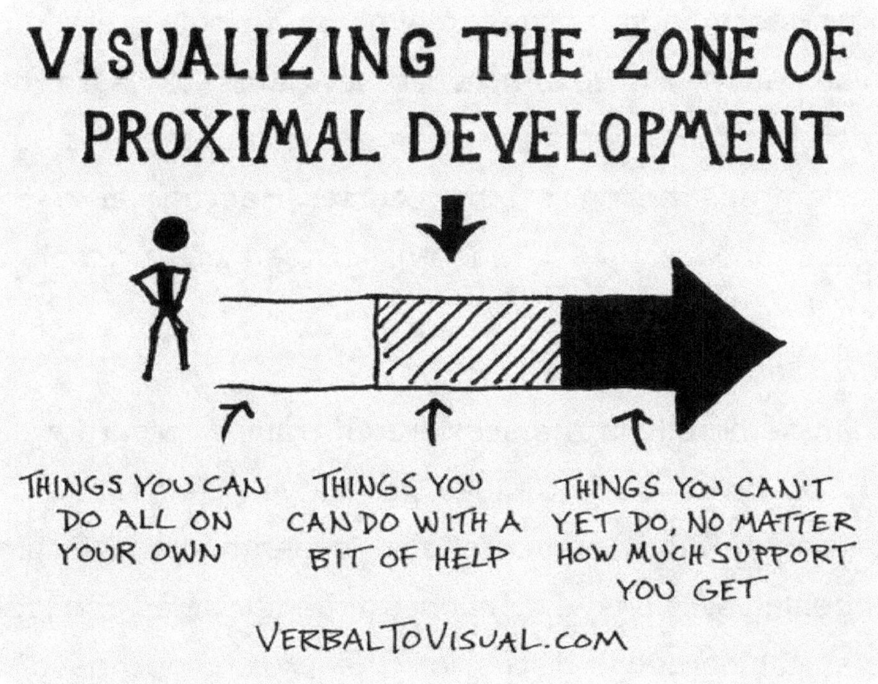

The pioneers of accelerated learning call it a must-have 21st-century skill. Our era is that of dynamic change and speed. Every single moment unveils a series of newer skills and opens doors to previously unknown facts. Time is money here, speed is its currency. Therefore educators of accelerated learning focus on applying multi-faceted learning techniques that involve all the sensory domains of development including cognitive, social, emotional and physical. They target the holistic learning and retention of knowledge. The acquirer of the knowledge through this method is presented with alternative ways to learn the same information, not just relying on a single method of presentation. For example, if he wants to learn the process of gardening and he has opted for the accelerated version of the course. He can learn the process in a couple of months instead of a year-long course.

How? You may ask.

When he enrolls in the accelerated training program, he will be given opportunities to actively participate in learning through presentations, experiments, practical gardening sessions, excursions to the nurseries and local botanical gardens, discussing the pros and cons of a particular seeding method during group discussions, presenting his analysis on a particular research material on tropical plants. He would be able to grasp even the more in-depth topics such as comparing the effects of certain fertilizers on the level of toxicity of the soil, by plotting a statistical graph after studying past data. All this would be possible because, in this program, he would be letting the information come in through various channels, keeping an open mind, and following an integrated approach to learning. Thus strengthening the memory and completing the acquisition of knowledge happens in the shortest time period possible.

Sometimes another term for accelerated learning is used interchangeably, i.e. *mind hacking.* Even though the former is more like a goal to be achieved while the latter is one of the methods to achieve it. Experts state that learning is a part of development and development is not a linear process, it occurs by leaps and bounds. The following graph can show this concept a little more visually.

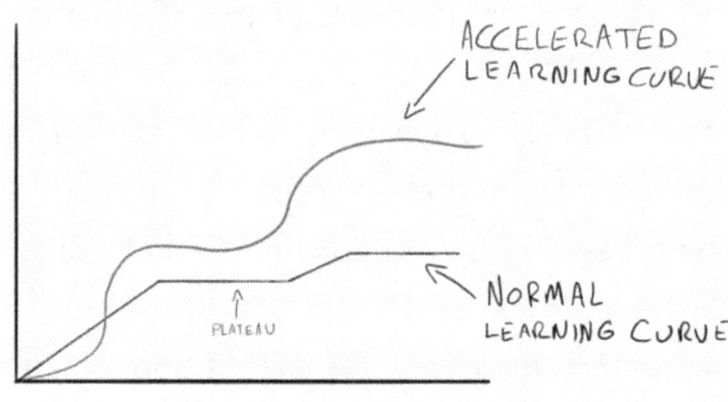

DARIUS FOROUX

Learning with acceleration focuses on not only *what* a thing is, but *how* it works too, at the same time. By taking the initiative in learning, the learner develops a *want to* attitude instead of *having to* mindset. Referring back to the term *mind hacking,* one can say that it a process of meta-learning where your brain is literally reprogrammed and reconditioned to function in a certain way. Your brain needs to be aware of the way *you* want it to work instead of the way it functions on an auto-pilot mode.

Multiple Intelligences and your Neural Learning Model:

Howard Gardener, a renowned American psychologist of educational and development, proposed his theory about evidence of multiple talents possessed by every human. The tendency of a person to be skilled at multiple things makes the concept of intelligence quite vast. It broadens the possibility of improvement and boosts the confidence of even the most average of students. A person can be good at wordplay, *or* physical sport, *or* music, *or* creative art, *or* cooking, *or* math, etc. Or he can be a jack of all and these talents can be present in him concurrently. In that case, we can replace those *"or"* with *"and"*, can't we?

Similarly, the neural programming model suggests that a person may be more of a visual nature, or a lingual one, or an audio-visual one, etc. This means that some people are more sensitive to what they perceive graphically rather than what they listen to or speak of. This makes them more visual in nature and a similar approach should be adopted while presenting them with memory improvement techniques or accelerated learning activities.

For example, they would be more interested in watching a short graphical documentary on a particular topic than reviewing an informative but textual article about it in a magazine. A lingual person, however, would be eager to swallow up the whole book in order to learn information on a given topic. But if he was assigned making of an info graph or creating a chart to summarize what he has learned, he may find it a chore. Therefore, assessing yourself to know which sort of behavior model your mind follows, is an important prerequisite to adapting a particular learning strategy or memory boosting method.

Speed Reading

Speed reading is one of the strategies of accelerated learning. It is the ability to quickly scan the printed words visually rather than *sub vocalizing* them in your mind. This means that you are not going to read the text to yourself or mumble them. Instead, you will take the images, quickly run your eyes over them to grasp the full sentence and keep moving forth.

What happens when you subvocalize?

Sub vocalizing means to utter the text in your mind i.e. with your inner voice. The biggest setback to reading quickly is focusing too much on the comprehension. Many people tend to repeat a sentence a couple of times in their mind to understand more while attempting to read quickly too. This contradicts the speed.

What happens is that your brain is working every single nanosecond of the time. It never stops. When you read a word mentally, it is taken as a new task. A message is sent to the brain to encode it, while your eyes are also at work to see the letters that form the word and the phonetic sounds that are combined to articulate that word even if only as an inner voice. A series of messages are sent and received in a short span of time and occupy your mind thus slowing down the reading process. Instead, if you avoid subvocalizing, your brain will directly encode the text as visual images and show you what they are and how they look to help you recognize them quickly. Just like when you *see* a tree, you will *recognize* it as a tree if you have *seen* it before.

An average person can read around 200 words per minute without practicing speed reading skills. But skilled speed-readers tend to accomplish a speed for reading about 400 or more words per minute. Almost double of what an average reader does. Sometimes they even reach 700-1000 wpm range through repeated practice and determination.

The important thing is to understand when you should require speed reading and when you should opt for comprehensive reading. Usually, when you are researching for something you often must go through numerous papers and studies. The speed-reading techniques can prove to be handy here. However, always remember to maintain some semblance of the basic concept or argument being presented in the text that you are speed reading without spending too much time over analysis now. The time for review and analysis would come later when you prepare a critical summary.

We are listing some major points to remember while speed reading a text:

- *Avoid subvocalization:* Don't read to yourself.

- *Avoid visual regression:* Don't let your sight wander around the next page. Compel it to follow the train of the sentence with a finger or a tip of a pencil.

- *Avoid too much focus on comprehension*: Don't be caught up in visualizing the scenario you are reading about. Don't try to analyze it just now. Keep reading. You only have seconds to complete a sentence.

- *Avoid perceiving a certain collection of words as single units*: Try to catch them as augmented groups or phrases. Most words are used together in a group or universal phrase so often that you recognize them in an instant when you spot them on the page.

For e.g. when you see; "Looking forward to hearing from you", you can read it as a whole quickly. It is also a way to predict text, that is what Google often does while you compose an email. Similarly, the idioms like, "beating around the bush", can be taken as a complete unit too.

- *Avoid reading linearly (line by line)*: Read the first and the last sentence of each paragraph before taking a quick snapshot of the middle. The opening sentence will usually tell you what will be covered in the following paragraph and the last sentence will provide you with the crux.

- *Push yourself to read faster:* Don't settle for less, be ambitious. Push your limits to extend further, aim higher. If you are managing to read at 400 words per minute speed, aim for 450 wpm as your next target. When you start managing 450 wpm, aim for 500 wpm instead. Force your eyes to move quicker than they are moving currently.

Remember, accelerated learning techniques are all about a psycho-emotional mindset. Your emotions, behavior, and intention, they all matter a lot when it comes to achieving improvement in targeted results.

Chapter7: Mind Programming, an Insight

Programming is basically used in computer science as an act of designing a set of instructions to be executed by a computer. A computer program is a set of instructions which tells the computer what to do and how to process. If it were not for these carefully designed and structured programs, the computer would have been just a physical body of useless hardware without a functional brain. *Mind programming* is usually referred to as an act of structured encoding of information that can be controlled and executed in an organized manner *willfully*.

The above explanation of computer programming can be applied in this context as well. As the mind absorbs information, it needs structured, systematic instructions to process this information. This is where programming is needed. Studies have linked the process of mind programming to both individual and collective settings. Experts state that the mind is not just an individual's tool for thought. It is much more complex than that. The mind can be a medium for communication between individuals.

It can be a sponge that absorbs external impressions and environmental vibes along with its own collection of internal thoughts and emotions. It works as an implicit as well as an explicit channel of interaction. However, it should be used to control the chaotic thought process, instead of controlling other people. It should be more about regaining focus on your own responses and behavior, instead of manipulating others' reactions.

Many of you have heard a word being frequently used in wordy speeches and marketed content; *"result-oriented"*. Have you ever wondered how the notion started? There is something called thinking backward i.e. top to bottom. Normal, average people may start a task from the bottom, working hard to pass the milestones to achieve the goal. Mind programmers would First jump to the top, imagining the ultimate result of each particular course of action they might take. Then they will travel backward in their thinking to trace the possible pathways that would have led to that result, ultimately reaching the bottom starting point to realize what should be their first course of action to reach the desired goal or result.

Similarly, unleashing the astonishing powers of mind by repeated practices and training sessions, what once can eventually control is the ability to overcome challenging situations and remain steadfast in stormy life weather. He can be unfazed in front of turbulent waves of uncertain circumstances. Mind programming has an innate concept of *mind over matter.* This principle skill suggests that no matter what you encounter in life your mental strength, determination, and stoic ability can make you have the upper hand on the situation and let the *steering wheel of your mind* handle the *vehicle of your body*. Minding something literally means *to "remember and pay attention to."* If you think something is important enough to be noticed, you not only pay extra attention to it but make a conscious effort to remember it as well. Paying attention and making a conscious effort is the key to mind programming. When you hear something like; *By having optimistic thoughts, you will meet positive results.* You might doubt the authenticity of such a statement. However, it can be true because what you *convince* your mind to think is what it eventually compels you to act upon. Your actions are mostly driven by your ambitions and your outlook on life has a powerful grip on your decision-making mechanism.

"Don't convince your body, convince your mind."

The more you open the windows of your mind, the more open your eyes will be to the secrets of a successful life. Now the question is, are there really windows in your mind? What sort of windows are they?

Actually, in a strictly biological sense, you have those windows as sensory channels through which your sensory organs take in information and your brain processes it so that you may learn about new things. However, by keeping an open mind you let all the possible tracks for making new mental connections or rebuilding the older ones, become traceable.

Sometimes the idea thoughts as invisible beings sound quite daunting but it also makes us capable of possessing something that is only ours. The personal forces inside our brain that can be our treasure alone, easily attainable, and durably appreciable. No one can fight us for possession of this treasure. No one can even see our weapon for winning the battles of our life. This can make us lead an independent, powerful life. Though modern studies have devised quite a few methods to read the mind and unveil its hidden treasures, there is still a long way to go before it becomes a completely transparent container.

Still, thoughts can no longer be considered a matter of abstract reality. For even your own understanding you must perceive them as manageable packets or blocks of information or intention that can be classified into colors, or images, or objects, or symbols, or letters, or numbers, or even food items! Whatever you choose them to be in order to organize them in clearly defined categories or compartments. This is what personality modeling or thinking styles classification, an important aspect of mind programming teaches us.

According to some thinking, styles vary according to personality traits. First, you must identify your personality model in order to identify how your thinking processes. There is content galore on the subject of self-help and soft skills mastery. These books explain behavior models and are the tips given in them are often based on the characteristic personality models. For example, modern job interviews and selection screening tests are often designed to contain at least some questions that assess the personality of the candidate by measuring the quotient of his id, ego, superego, as described by the famous psychoanalyst and neurologist, Sigmund Freud. This is because emotional intelligence is considered as much important as academic excellence in the recent era. The *id, ego, and superego* are three structures of personality that can be instrumental in assessing your personality behavior and model. This, in turn, would be helpful in programming your mind. These personality elements determine the nature of your behavior while resolving various conflicts that arise at every stage of life. Id, Ego, and Superego are depicted in the info graph below.

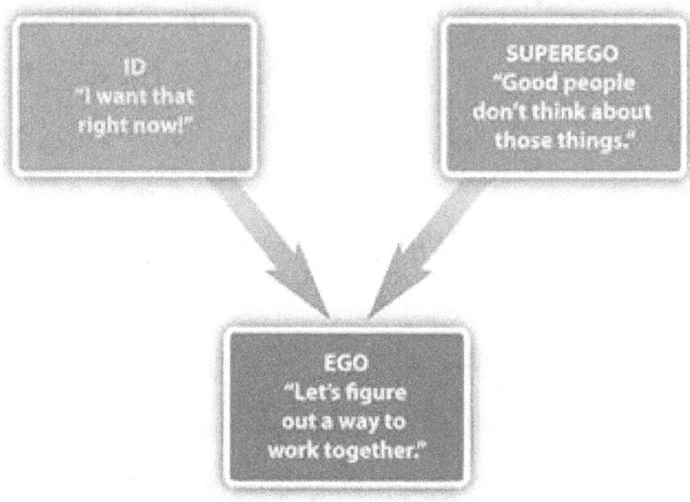

The focus of this book was not to let *others* understand *your* mind's power, but let *you* gain insight on how to have a mindset that can improve your thinking style and memory capacity. Therefore, we have described mostly about how mind programming works for an individual's personal improvement.

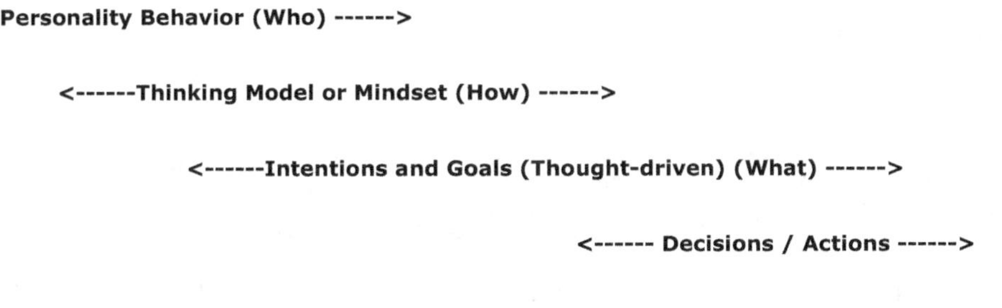

The term actively used nowadays with respect to mind programming is *mind hacking* which is actually the shortcut method for the former. While the latter may achieve some progress by accelerated training and, it may not reach the profound mental layers and personality issues, thus being effective for only a short term. While careful mind programming achieves long term results and a complete restructuring of the mental schemas.

There is often a concept of classical and operant conditioning involved in these training sessions. *Accommodation* and *adaptation* are also practices to ensure maximum learning and restructuring of mental schemas.

What is schema

In cognitive psychology, a schema refers to a set of information or encrypted code associated with a particular experience. When a person encounters a situation, the way he reacts during it marks an impression in mind and in response to this stimulus a schema is organized. Now if a person reacts the same way again in a similar situation, this schema will be maintained and newer experience will be added as well in the same set of mental structures. However, if that person reacts in a different manner the next time the same situation occurs, the schema will be altered or discarded to be replaced by the new information that is generated for a different response to a particular stimulus. When the old schema is removed to make room for or to *accommodate* a new experience, *accommodation* occurs. Whereas, if the old schema is maintained with little or no changes, and similar experiences are being *added* to just update the existing cognitive structure, *assimilation* occurs.

To review these concepts in a little more detail, let us quickly answer the following questions:

What is classical conditioning

Being one of the learning procedures which determine the way our mind works, controlling the way we think and act, classical conditioning is a behavioral psychology phenomenon, presented by Russian physiologist Ivan Pavlov. Also referred to as an automated or associative type of learning, classical conditioning lets the mind learn a certain response or behavior by automatically associating one stimulus with the other with or without any distinctive relationship between the two.

For e.g. At the start of a lesson, when you often see your teacher take out an attendance sheet each time she enters the class, you would automatically consider or *assume* any piece of paper in her hand as an attendance sheet expecting your roll call. But maybe the next time she takes out the first paper upon arriving in the class, it could be your recent test report instead of an attendance sheet.

What happens is in normal circumstances you may not expect any sheet of paper to be an attendance sheet or if you meet the same teacher after school near the parking you will not expect her to start calling your name for attendance, but if it is the *start of a lesson, and that particular teacher carrying a sheet in her hand*, you would expect it to be the roll call because your mind has become conditioned to produce a similar response each time these two stimuli are presented to you together in a certain setting. Most of the phobias such as fear for fire and emotions of anxiety, anticipation, boredom, nausea, etc. are triggered by associating certain surroundings (stimulus 1) with certain objects or smells (stimulus 2), etc.

A person who was burned by a candle flame in a dark room may start fearing both the candle and the darkness. A person who feels the urge to vomit every time he sees blood in the hospital may have nausea when he sees a hospital room even when there is no apparent display of blood. However, most of the time these behavior patterns get conditioned only through reinforcement. Therapies in mind training sessions can be conducted to make the previous behavior extinct but extinction is not particularly translated to forgetting a memory, instead, it means that newer experiences replace the older ones, therefore new learning occurs.

What is operant conditioning

A remarkable contribution to the behavioral conditioning theory is the operant conditioning given by B.F. Skinner. It is a type of associative learning that is more controlled than the classical conditioning to achieve the desired outcome. In contrast to the classical conditioning, operant conditioning operates on the principle of conditioning the desired response in a person by revealing the possible consequences of his certain behavior in each situation. This ensures the achievement of positive learning outcomes through a concept of reward and punishment. For e.g. A learner associates his scoring high in a quiz (desired behavior or response) with getting no-homework pass or best-student badge (reward). So if the teacher wants to improve the student behavior, she conditions them by letting them know the possible consequences of how they respond. Through repetitions or reinforcements, encouragement or discouragement, a particular good or bad behavior can be strengthened or weakened respectively.

What is the accommodation?

Altering the mental environment in order to make a suitable room for new information. Here, the old responses prototyped in the existing mental schema to certain experiences are not consistent with the new ones so they must be replaced by a new schema to accommodate the new information. Mastering the way mental schema is patterned leads us to get the knack of mind programming. The very term called *prototype* in the context of programming means that structuring of mind is indeed what lays at the heart of mind power.

What is assimilation?

Adjusting new information in an existing schema to be in sync with the older experiences. To assimilate is to understand the new information based on past experiences. Assimilation is actually the foundational pillar for experiential learning. It is also the concept through which many sequential forms of academics are taught in schools. The term *prerequisite* is the derivative of this very idea of assimilation that shapes the mental schema or cognitive structure in our mind. This state of mind suggests stability or equilibrium that ensures smooth learning. However, sometimes accommodation is needed instead of assimilation to let the innovation, creativity, and dynamics enter the static stream of mind.

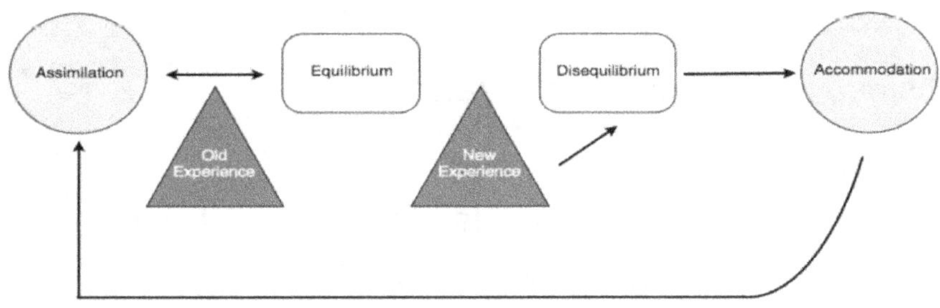

The Law of Attraction in Mind Programming

The dynamics of mind programming include several inspiring concepts and motivational outlook on life obtained through the powers of mind. The law of attraction is one of those extremely inspiring concepts that has a very positive vibe to it.

"The imaginable is achievable"

If you can consider your mind having magnetic power, you can imagine your desired results automatically being attracted to your optimistic thoughts carried by your magnetic mind. What you think is what you become or what becomes of you.

Consider these tips for reference:

- ✓ Avoiding mental laziness and procrastination is one of the keys to unlock successful outcomes.

- ✓ Have a pep talk with your inner self each time you feel negative thoughts swarming in your mind.

- ✓ Reward yourself on your hard work when you perform well. It can be anything from a cheat day incorporated in your diet or a simple compliment to yourself and no, it is not against modesty. Believe that you deserve it.

✓ Don't underestimate yourself, don't overestimate too. Set realistic goals but try to expand your potential by positive self-encouragement.

✓ Intend moderately but act generously to pursue the unwavering thought.

✓ Having confidence in your intentions can make the process of the proceeding actions easier. The mind focuses on the goal post, the body on the playground.

Chapter8: Life Skills for Memory Improvement

The famous pioneer of the Montessori Method of Education, an Italian Doctor Maria Montessori says:

> *"All victories and all human progress are dependent on the strength that comes from within."*

Progress is most often built on the obvious, existing things that we overlook in our quest for hidden secrets of success. We perceive self-help as an out of the world training, even though it most certainly is an inner motivational concept. Our life is shaped by the way we *live* it. By changing the way of our existing lifestyle, we can improve the living standard exponentially. If you take sufficient sleep, eat healthily, and socialize with nice company, you can achieve a kind of stability in life that helps you relax and let your brain gain more focus.

Nowadays, the concept of life skills is getting all the necessary hype and duly so. Gone are the days when leisure activities were just pass-times and habits just a routine. Eating, sleeping, communicating, socializing, exercising, all these are counted as skills now. They are taught in personality development centers specially dedicated to groom you and organize your mentality to make use of these life skills. However, you don't specifically need to get enrolled in an institution to learn these skills that aid in increasing your brainpower and improve your memory.

Yoga & Exercise

Muscles are known as *instruments of movement,* so described by Dr. Maria Montessori. She says that the will in our mind is implemented by the muscles in our body. Hence the relationship between mental and physical processes is vital for development. Inactivity and sedentary lifestyle dictate exhaustive mind labor dissociated from the active muscles, eventually increasing the immobility in mind as well. If the body is not trained for physical labor the mind will suffer in correcting the mistakes made by the body and the struggle that it may go through upon encountering any physical challenge. Yoga and exercises such as walking, running, skipping, swimming, etc. not only help to activate the muscular system by increasing the blood flow but also help to alleviate stress and depression. The relaxed mind is, therefore, able to remember more and retain it longer.

The practice of yoga basically originated from India as an orthodox principle school of complementary medicine. Old Indian yogic practices suggest that yoga can be used to increase motion range, core strength, physical flexibility, and mental focus. It can be a perfect mood improvement therapy which can also be an elemental practice in disease prevention.

There is a famous and interesting concept in authentic Indian yogic scriptures which state that the human body has amazing latent energy stored in its core or spinal column. The air that we breathe enhances the recharging power of the electrical potential present in our brain matter. Even the way we breathe through our left or right nostrils affect the way our internal body heat is increased or decreased. Each time we breathe through the right nostril, energy in the form of oxygen increases the blood flow to the brain and positive charge is produced and stored in the brain cells. A time comes when positive energy reaches a peak level so that we tend to breathe through our left nostril automatically. This time negative charge is produced and stored until it reaches the peak level too. Again the breathing alternates from left nostril to the right nostril. This alternate transition makes a path for the current to pass from positive to negative and vice versa which in turn, produces the electricity that flows along with the blood reaching different parts of the body.

The produced electricity is stored as a latent potential inside the vertebral column because of the presence of some brain matter in the spinal cord, as it is also a major part of our nervous system. When this potent electrical energy is revived or recharged through regular practice and yoga sessions, it passes through the core, reaching the brain and revitalizing the brain cells one by one. The major activation of nervous chips in the computer-like circuitry of our brain opens a series of wondrous revelations for a person. It gives him a new perspective of things, new thoughts, and ideas that can be instrumental in bringing out his optimum potential and improvement in his memory skills. This is ordinary people are stimulated and trained to achieve great things in life.

Meditation and Mindfulness

They say when *no one speaks, the mind does.* Meditation is to the psyche what physical workout is to the body. It is a mind training method to gain focus and concentration. Mindful meditation is a type of meditation where you train your mind to focalize on a singular thought process. This increases the ability to concentrate, avoid unnecessary distractions, and improve memory. When you are focused on life, you achieve bigger things. Reflection is the primary principle of meditation. To meditate as a beginner;

- o Select a peaceful environment to sit.
- o Make yourself in a comfortable position, relaxing your posture.
- o Close your eyes.
- o Take a deep breath carefully focusing on your inhalation and exhalation.
- o Let your mind speak to you.
- o Listen to the thoughts and reflect.

- o Open your eyes after an initial 10-15 minutes session.
- o Practice daily.

Sleeping well

Sleep is not just a way of going into oblivion, but a way to refuel your brain. Sleep lets your otherwise busy brain to relax and focus on detoxification of the nervous system. Even the metabolism in your body works better during rest periods. The blood flow is better during sleep and the energy level is restored. Sleep deprivation causes harmful toxin production inside your brain and hinders the mental processes. The adverse effects of too much wakefulness without adequate sleep, include obesity, memory decline, metabolic imbalance, hypertension, early death risks and several other health concerns due to the weakened immune system. The happy hormone, *serotonin* is said to be a precursor agent in *melatonin* formation, the latter is said to be actively produced in the darkness of night, helping you to regulate your inner biological clock. Melatonin is also responsible for maintaining your sleep-wake cycles. This makes it evident that sleeping at night is very important in organizing your routine. Together, both serotonin and melatonin play an important role in regularizing your appetite, sleep, and behavioral patterns.

Eating Healthy

Healthy nutrition is one of the most important milestones to be achieved in your journey towards memory improvement. Healthy food choices can positively affect your behavior and thought process along with maintaining your body's functionality. For instance, when you are hungry you feel quite cranky and when you eat a lot you feel sluggish or drowsy. Unhealthy patterns of eating should be avoided to gain stability in life. The food supplements to improve your mental capability and contribute to your overall physical health have been discussed in detail at the end of this book.

Smiling and Socializing

Dopamine along with serotonin is released when a person smile. Both neuro transmitting chemicals travel inside the brain letting your nerves know about your smile and the brain becomes happy to see you in a happy mood!

The benefits of a smile can be enough to make an encyclopedia out of it. Here we are just relating it to your brain activity as is the purpose of this book.

Socializing is an art of living. Information is the primary subject of your memory and most of it comes from interaction. When you interact, you meet new people, accumulate new ideas, get inspiration to change your outlook, gather various topics in your mind to ponder upon. In short, you gather a wealth of cognitive intelligence through socialization. You gather food for thought. You become used to remembering people, their conversations, their opinions, etc.

Can you imagine a mind becoming powerful and capable of memory enhancement when the person bearing that mind is always alone, isolated from the outer world? Imagine your mind becoming a closed-door room, with closed windows, becoming void of oxygen, filled with the stale smell. It is slow brain death. Smile and socialize to give your mind proper ventilation. Take a breather!

Walking Backwards

Yes, you heard it right! Walking backward is not a play, it is a carefully planned, conscious activity to stimulate mental performance. Apart from its physical benefits, it can also help in getting the attention of your mind due to the unusual movement of the body. As your body is going against the normal nature of walking, each step is to be taken with mental consciousness. This compels your brain to remain actively attentive. These sorts of unusual practices must be incorporated periodically in your routine exercise or as an early morning brain warm-up activity. It helps ensure the reconstruction of an otherwise usual, routine to avoid monotony. The brain becomes so conditioned at procedural routines that it goes on an auto mode. To jerk it out of that boring, lethargic mode, an unpredictable activity is needed to sharpen and improve the memory focus.

Chapter9:   Alternative   Natural Therapies for Memory Improvement

The happiness of enjoying sound health is invaluable. Nothing can replace it. The human body is like a highly functional, busily active working complex. Each department is dedicated to a particular aspect of the business. Every day is full of a hectic schedule, busy with work overflow. There are many floors in this business complex or building. Each floor has a special purpose of serving. There is a food production area or pantry. There is a sewerage maintenance floor. Then there is ventilation or air quality maintenance system as well. One floor has a smooth transport system used is entirely for communication management and logistics between all the other floors. The top floor is higher authority supervisory committee, heading the overall processing of the business.

The simulated example above can provide a clearer picture of how integrated our body is, how hectic the daily work of food energy processing, respiration, excretion, blood circulation can be. How it makes the work of the brain harder, as all the functions are eventually supervised and controlled by the brain. This all integration of working floors needs perfect coordination and control. Brain health must be in a sound position to make the work smoother.

The human body has an active flow of electricity inside it just like batteries have an electric flowing inside them. All the nervous system is coordinated by the smooth transmission of electric impulses or signals from channel to channel, as discussed on some occasions in previous chapters. The signals once traveled on a particular channel leave a memory trace in their wake. As our brain is composed of both white and gray matter, its shape is quite like the inside of a walnut. This bi-colored matter is a special battery-like structure, conductive for electric signals. Through the proper supply of oxygen and nutrition, the batteries of the brain get recharged. More details of how this electricity in the brain is actually produced and how it gets recharged will be discussed under the topic of *Acupressure* or *Reflexology*.

Acupressure, Acupuncture & Reflexology

Neurological research suggests that brain cells are structured in such a concrete manner that they are quite protected inside the nervous system, recharging them or reviving them takes quite a lot of effort. However, some complementary alternative medicine has provided remedial methods to revive them and prevent them from becoming depleted debris, sometimes referred to as brain-sand. Most of the calcified, hardened debris accumulates in the pineal gland inside the brain. This gland is mostly known for releasing melatonin, the sleep-regulating hormone that is stimulated in darkness. The pineal gland often referred to as *the third eye* in modern spiritual practices, is vital in mental relaxation and stress alleviation. Its detoxification is as important as recharging the depleting brain cells.

CAM (Complimentary Alternative Medicine) experts suggest that most of the disorders are caused by weakened brain cells and an increase in depleted cells' debris. This also weakens the flow in brain electricity which is essential or active functioning of the body. It is exactly like when an electronic toy cannot be operated on a dried-up battery cell and therefore stops functioning. Experts advise consuming charged metal (gold, copper, silver, etc.) water to help recharge the cells in the brain. Even the patients with paralysis, cancer, arthritis, etc. were treated using this water and showed positive improvement. It proves to be an energy tonic for the weakened mental state and anti-aging supplement.

The above details were given to give you an in-depth insight into the importance of the proper flow of electric current in your body and what consequences may result from the inability of brain cells to recharge. Adequate maintenance of the electricity flow can be possible by the Acupressure method. Acupressure is actually an ancient practice found years ago in India. *Devendra Vora* in his book about alternative therapies, *"Health in your hands"*, states that the practice wasn't duly preserved in India and therefore traveled afterward in the form of its variant called *Acupuncture,* from Ceylon to Japan and then

China. However Chinese claim that the practice was already prevalent in traditional Chinese medicine.

Acu means, "needle", pressure here indicates the method of applying firmly controlled pressure by fingers and thumb or an unpointed compress, on specific body points called acupoints that reflect certain areas of functionality. Acupuncture method, in contrast, uses piercing objects to treat specific illness points. Both practices are effective as the points on the body targeted to treat the diseases are more or less similar. The term reflexology is also sometimes used interchangeably with acupressure due to the same underlying principle of treatment though pressure reflexes. Acupuncture is mostly used to reach deep skin to treat the disease as it involves piercing and penetration whereas acupressure uses pressure on the surface to trigger the profound body parts.

The concept of acupressure is governed by bioelectricity. The negative energy or charge is *chen* while the positive energy or charge is chi. This electricity controls the five body elements known as, earth, space, fire, air, and water. These five elements are said to be represented by our five fingers of the hand. The paths for electric current to pass are called meridian channels that for the right side, go from right-hand fingers' tips to the right foot's toes. Similarly or the left side as well. The fitness depends upon proper current flow in these meridian channels. If due to some disease or toxification, blockage or stagnation occurs in the blood flow, the reflexive pressure technique helps resolve it. Many of the head nerves and brain acupoints are located in your feet and hands. For example, the left and right feet's toes and hands' thumbs are for brain stimulation and control. By applying pressure to these specific points, an electric current can be passed to the respective organ and activate it. The pressure can be accompanied by a sporadic massage technique at the targeted point area to help stabilize the pressure and blood flow.

Meditation & Prithvi Mudras in Acupressure points' combinations:

As mentioned before, the five fingers in our hands represent five basic elements of nature:

Thumb = Sun / Fire

Index = Air

Middle = Space / Sky

Ring = Earth

Small or pinky = Water

By pressing a combination of specific points on these fingers, elemental vibes can be controlled. Many diseases can be prevented and many positive effects on mental and physical health can be achieved. A mudra is a certain hand gesture or symbolic hand position that carries a spiritual meaning significant during meditation and yoga. It uses acupressure or reflexology principles to influence the energy flow.

The *meditation mudra* is simply posed by touching the index finger with the thumb. Do it with both hands while sitting with your back straight, preferably with closed eyes. You may or may not sit in a lotus position, however, the latter is effective for better results. Applying too much pressure is not needed, a subtly focused touch will do the trick.

Effects: It benefits the mind by increasing concentration, memory power, and insomniac tendencies.

The Prithvi Mudra is posed by putting your ring finger i.e. your fourth finger pressed to your thumb. Here also you can sit in a lotus posture to achieve better concentration.

Effects: It benefits the mind and body by regaining the lost strength, increasing the bio-electrical energy inside the body also known as life force or Chetna. This energy can induce a new vigor in an ailing mind-body system. It also helps recollect the peace of mind, enabling increased memory retention power.

These mudras can be practiced daily for 10-15 minutes as a beginner, then extended to half an hour at a later stage.

Cupping Therapy

Many of the people unfamiliar with alternative medicine therapies might not have heard about cupping therapy. However, the truth is that its history dates back to as early as 1550 BC. The people used it in Egypt and China in 5000 or so years ago. It was the most effective practice for treating several different ailments during the time of the Islamic empire. Cupping therapy is also known as *hijama* literally meaning *sucking* in Arabic. It is strongly recommended in Islam as a remedial practice for detoxification and universal healing. It is highly advised instead of fire cauterization methods. Extensively being practiced in the modern era, still, it is quite new to some people. Hijama therapy is advised to be practiced in the second half or third quarter of the month and generally before summers as monthly and annual detoxification rituals. Hijama should be done on an empty stomach so that the energy is vitalized towards the brain after the toxins are eliminated. That is why fasting is advised on middle specific dates 13th, 14th, and 15th, of every month.

What happens is that the body gets concentrated on cleaning up the toxins already inside the body, without having to focus on the additional nutrition process or digestion. Avoiding some meals by fasting in the day and eating by the end of the day (dusk) and before dawn can help metabolize the deposited fat and sugar and lower the cholesterol level. It will also help calm the body's aggression and blood rush that happens during a full moon. Ramadan fasting and another voluntary fasting which Muslims observe, along with being a religious practice is a good detoxification method also followed by various other people around the world.

According to *Islamic tradition,* the lunar calendar i.e. the Islamic calendar system holds an important role in following the cupping practice and fasting. People should know that the moon has instrumental effects on the earth residents and the environment. Being the closest satellite and previously a part of the earth's terrestrial body, moon not only affects the water bodies on the earth but the humans as well. This can be seen during full moon phases. The gravitational force of attraction causes the raising of tides in the water.

Every single thing on earth experiences a rush of energy and a pull towards a higher level. Even the blood in the human body is raised according to some alternative medicine pioneers. They say that the moon does affect human behavior and there is evidence of increased aggressiveness in schizophrenic patients during full moon cycles. The heightened tides coincide with heightened emotions. While the body's blood rush is at its peak, it waves up and pushes aside the toxic garbage, just like the ocean waves rage towards the beachside then revert back, leaving the flushed out waste in their wake. After the full moon starts waning, the toxins rushed towards the head settle down like sediments, gathered between the shoulder blades and the upper back region.

After that, the cupping is advised in the latter half of the month according to the Islamic healing philosophy specifically on the 17th, 19th, and 21st of each month. This helps the brain to concentrate on the cleaning up, collecting the already accumulated dead cell debris and toxic chemicals inside the body. Several of the hijama cupping therapy points involve the treatment of serious diseases. Hijama is also very effective in improving the memory. There are specific points serve this purpose. After applying subtle incisions, suction is done through appropriate glass or plastic cups or a specialized pressure/suction gun.

Ayurvedic Tips

The Ayurveda is an Indian medical system. It has a wealth of text showing years of research about different types of food items and spices, their respective nutrients and their effects or after-effects on health. There is a general principle stating that:

Heat is life, cold is death. Eat or drink to preserve the fire or heat inside the body to help maintain the digestive system.

The *dosha* concept in Ayurveda explains the mind-body prototype. The person living an appropriate lifestyle according to his *dosha* can maintain a mentally and physically healthy life. The great herb *Gotu Kola* or *Indian Pennywort* used in the Ayurveda tradition is proven to be an effective brain booster. It is shown to increase the intellect, making learning easier and strengthening the memory too. There has been evidence of improvement on both animals and humans. This herb is also called Brahmi literal Hindi translation means; *"giving supreme knowledge".* You may use it as a memory-enhancing tonic by soaking the leaves overnight and then making a paste by grinding it with nuts, milk, and honey. It is very beneficial for nervous system improvement.

Aroma Therapy

Often called a holistic healing method, aromatherapy is used to treat illnesses by making use of natural extracts derived from plants. Due to its method of using essential oils as healing agents to promote health and wellness, aromatherapy is also called essential oils treatment. Aromatic oils are plant extracts obtained from the flowers, wood, leaves, and fruits, etc. They trigger the mind, body, and soul. Enhancing the senses and lifting the mood, relieving the ailing person from inner conflict and emotional stress.

As essential oils' potency is very high, instead of letting the patient directly smell them, the aromatherapy is done by diffusing the essential oils' aroma in an enclosed, quiet room. Either the diffusion is done by an electric diffuser or a manual one. While the aromatic atmosphere is created the person is prepared to take a massage in the aromatic room. The soothing fragrances when inhaled, calm the mind and the body and affects the neuro-limbic system. The massage can be a topical aroma-therapeutic method while the same scent can be inhaled internally as well. This region of the brain's nervous system is known to regularize the memory structures, emotional behavior, and endocrine function of the body.

The aromatherapy, although popular for beauty purposes in the modern era, it is in fact, one of the most effective cures for mental stress, anxiety, mood swings, memory decline, and emotional imbalance.

Some of the notable essential oils for mental health are listed below:

Sandalwood: Derived from the sandalwood tree, inhaling this oil can uplift the mood during meditation. It gives off a pleasant woody smell and is perfect for releasing tension. It is a memory improvement agent that helps relax the brain.

Bergamot: It has a citrus-smelling fragrance. It helps decrease the anxiety and depression levels. Hence, improving mental health.

Rosemary: It is an ideal catalyst to sharpen concentration and increase mental activity.

Tea tree oil: It can calm the mind. The soothing nature of the extract makes the inhaling person considerably lighter, more relieved.

Lemon: By boosting the defense mechanism, this citric oil can enhance the energy level and concentration. The heightened senses and increased focus can help prevent memory loss and other mental disorders.

Peppermint: A refreshing fragrance oil, peppermint gives instant energy to the inhaling person. It relieves headaches, nauseous feelings, and stress. Research shows that reasoning power, thinking skills, and attention span can be improved by inhaling the peppermint oil.

Lavender: It has a special calming effect. It can improve the insomniac concerns and help to relax the mind, enhancing the cognitive skills further.

Jasmine: Carrying a sweetly infectious scent, this essential oil can boost the metabolism, libido, and is also helpful in boosting brain activity by reducing anxiety and stress.

Chamomile: chamomile tea is quite famous for its relaxing quality. The chamomile essential oil can alleviate sleep deprivation, anxiety, and a dampened mood.

Art Therapy

Art therapy is a beautifully effective way of self-expression and channelization of inner thoughts, ideas, and conflicts. Leading to a stabilized balance between the brain hemispheres, the integration of emotional externalization and internal mind notions, brings out an encouraging effect on the overall health. The art therapy is proven to be an influential trigger for the activation of dormant memories and lost experiences especially in patients suffering from Alzheimer's. Art therapy is a form of psychotherapeutic remedial process that uses artistic techniques to treat psychological disorders. The creative process not only is explorative self-discovery, but it also increases self-confidence and a sense of purpose in life.

Color Therapy or Chromotherapy

An interesting way of treating health issues, color therapy is done by inducing effects of different colors on the mind and the body. By vibes emitting out of swirling colors in a color therapy session, a holistic remedial approach is adapted to maintain the inner system of the body. To make these sessions a sensory experience, we need to perceive the colors as wavelengths that are interpreted by our brain through the retina, the human eye camera. This makes the experience more enhanced in terms of sensations and perception. The wavelengths in the colors are stimulators for electrifying the nerve impulses responsible for the smooth working of several biochemical processes in the brain.

This therapy can be done in various ways. Sometimes it is combined with aromatic oil diffusion technique to increase the focus while multiple specific colored fabrics are applied on your body. Sometimes different colored lights are illuminated to be reflected across the room where the person is sitting. Sometimes this light projection on the body may be accompanied by a massage on specific body points. Mostly shades of indigo and violets project a peaceful, calming effect. Green is closer to nature, helps purify the toxic nature of the body while red is more energizing if used moderately. The yellow is said to be a noticeable color, stimulating the nervous system. Due to its flashy and highlighted tone, yellow is considered a happy color that relieves the stress and depression. Experts in complementary medicine suggest that a combination of magnet therapy and color therapy on fingers helps in memory improvement. The blue environment in a room can help trigger creative skills in brainstorming tasks while a red-colored environment can boost the potential for memory retrieval.

Although there are some contradictions, still color therapy is reportedly an alternative treatment achieving positive results in many affected people. The right color combination can achieve powerfully instrumental contrast, which enables memory retention and cutthroat thinking skills. However, researches are still being conducted to gain further insight into this unusual but useful practice.

Chapter10: Effects of Life Experiences on Brain and Memory

John is a healthy child, starting school. His parents are both working to provide him a perfect home and his teachers are trying their best to make the school environment an extension of his home. His family wants to see him growing with sound health and positive memories. Hence they are trying to act as good role models for him, avoiding rows or even verbal sparring in front of him. They are creating a breathable atmosphere for him where he can grow happily, eagerly collecting the pleasant memories and cherishing them well. How john's parents can ensure or expect that their kid will become a happy man once he grows up?

The answer to this question can be deduced as a result of various scientific studies involving brain development. These studies suggest that the way our brain starts developing from childhood and to adulthood and afterward largely depends upon the early life experiences that we have encountered throughout our childhood and youth. These experiences become engraved in our mind's console. Each similar experience or incident can trigger the flashback or an associated feeling of a long-forgotten incident that happened in early childhood. A man who has been bitten by a dog in his early years as a child may demonstrate an abnormal fear for dogs even after he reaches his 60's. A kitchen maid who can work for hours cleaning the countertops, doing dishes, scouring floor tiles, rubbing the stoves, may not be as inclined to light up the stove with a matchstick. Why? Because she had burnt her hand by a lighter accidentally when she was a toddler. These feelings die hard. Too hard to discard. They remain in the subconscious part of the mind like lurking shadows of the past.

Coming back to John's case, his parents are trying to protect his childhood by getting influenced by any sort of neglect or negative experiences. They want him to not only develop physically or academically but socially and emotionally as well. Emotional development is as much an integral part of brain development as cognitive development. That is why modern psychology insists on emotional intelligence as an important personality development trait and essentially a life skill.

It is a known fact that the brain continues to develop even after birth. Development is a phenomenon of overall maturation of the cells of the body including both the size and the function. Some research evidence points to the concept of an increase in brain size during development. However, results of maltreated children neurological tests state a shocking revelation i.e. Children with negative experiences were left with a small size of brain matter, while stress-free children with positive, healthy experiences continued to have increased brain volume.

Scolding, bullying, abuse, and neglect, can cause the brain to focus more on self-protection and expression of basic personal needs. Hence in his quest to getting his needs fulfilled and his basic rights acknowledged, a child may invest too much energy in this aim. His brain may put essential skills such as cognitive development and communication skills at the back burner because it is too busy trying to be able to survive in society first. Not only will the self-esteem of the child suffer in this entire struggle, but he also becomes an introvert, shying away from the world, getting locked in his shell to protect himself from harsh behavior, criticism, and indifferent attitude of adults. His energies would all be singularly consumed in one basic domain of development and that too, in a limited way. Thus his brain potential for further growth and development in other important domains such as social, cognitive, physical, moral, language, etc. would be crushed. Here we can refer to Maslow's hierarchy of human needs graphically represented by a pyramid where each preceding stage of human needs must be fulfilled for a person to advance to the next level.

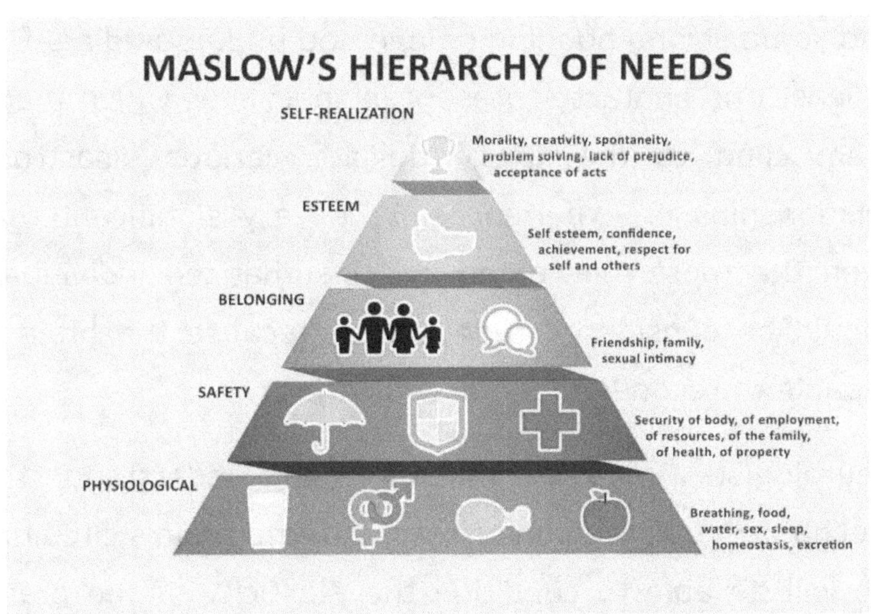

According to research, genetic expressions are all dependent upon the nature of life experiences one has undergone from infancy to maturity. While positive experiences switch the genes *on,* negative experiences can have an adverse effect on turning the genes *off.* This may result in perfectly normal children growing up becoming abnormal or showing at least some symptoms of mental disorder. Some of you may argue that people who regardless of going through several hurdles in their early life became eventually able to cope with them later on. Maybe because of therapies or mind training or meditation techniques. But the truth of the fact is, if we closely look into their background, we might be able to find some strong bonding of love and understanding with at least one character present in their lives which made them cling to the sanity despite various disastrous relationships or experiences. It is very significant that even the most maltreated and traumatized individuals should be considered redeemable because the brain is capable of reconditioning and rewiring.

Neurologists suggest that if can understand the mechanism of wiring and rewiring of the brain's circuitry, we will be able to condition the plasticity of the brain. This will help mind trainers devise strategies and therapies to reconnect the disconnected synaptic links in the brain which act as *windows of opportunity for learning.* This way, even the most deprived person can have an opportunity to relive the missed normal, happy experiences that can still have a positive effect on his life due to these reopened windows of opportunity or rewired neural connections. In terms of brain development and intellectual wealth, lost potential is far too detrimental a risk to be taken lightly. Therefore, stability of mind, memory, and emotions on the part of each member of the society play a vital role in the stability of human behavior, social normalcy, and overall human development index.

Chapter11: Foods and other Edible Supplements as Brain and Memory Boosters:

Do you imagine your brain as a separate living entity? Even if you don't, start doing it now!

Your brain is the driving force behind every action and emotion of yours. Your heart doesn't carry feelings, *your brain does.* Your heart pumps blood, while your brain deals with all your baggage. Stress, loneliness, failure, desperation, boredom, hyperactivity, and several other messy emotions are frequent visitors to your mind. That is the main reason, the subject of psychology is the human mind, not the heart.

What your body needs to relax and energize, your brain needs it double in amount. While you derive your body's vitality from food and nutrition, you tend to forget an important master organ of that body that is the powerhouse of all organs, *your brain.* You must feed those vital nutrients to enhance their performance. Remember, if you have a strong mind, you will ultimately have a strong body due to that mental strength present inside your mind pushing you to be healthy.

✓ Focus on what your diet *lacks* more than what your diet *should have.*

Consuming a healthy diet to vitalize your body is easy when it comes to selecting nutrient-rich vegetables and cereals. But focusing on *how to vitalize your brain too,* often becomes an overlooked concept. Nature has an interesting way of growing fruits and vegetables that are vital for our body organs. If we pay attention, we can discover how most of the nutritional fruits and vegetables resemble the shape of our body organs. For instance, Almonds for eyes, Walnut for brain, Apple for heart, Grapes (resembling pulmonary air sacs or alveoli) for lungs, Pears (/ Banana / Peru / similar) for ovaries.

Similarly, in the context of our topic, nature has bestowed us with a wealth of edible bounties that possess astonishing potential to improve brain activity and memory retention. For a keen eye and determined mind, the shut doors of the world open up to reveal several brain-boosting herbs and foods that can be a real gamechanger.

As you consume your diet, energy is produced by break down of the complex dietary substances into simpler particles. This energy is required to keep you functioning. Almost a whole quarter of that energy is utilized by your brain to cater to various functional processes while the rest is distributed among the remaining organs. Most of the nutritional energy is needed to enable you to interact with people, keep your emotions in check, and handle your day to day experiences. To facilitate this, your brain cells are always talking with each other.

Many of the *Integrative Nutritionists* suggest that our brain is a network of chemicals (neurotransmitters) flowing around via neural pathways. The level of cognitive power depends on the nature of chemicals' behavior. When you consume something, each morsel in your diet has some sort of chemical energy which can positively or negatively react with the chemicals of your brain. Maximum cognitive performance can be attained by consuming the right chemicals in the right amount.

Plant-derived oils and serums, remedial drinks, energy boosters, nutty treats, herbal extracts, etc. They all are a bunch of effective brain-boosting food. Studies prove that most of the ingredients in our food consist of plants and vegetables. Herbs were also a major part of edible medicinal products. This fact inspired a more detailed foray into the nature and composition of plants' bodies. Results show that the chemicals inside a plant react well with the brain chemicals to help increase the efficacy of several brain functions. They complement the chemicals interacting inside your brain, providing a necessary supplement, like leverage, to boost up the process where it slows down.

The Science behind it

During mind processing, neurotransmitters working inside the brain are mostly proteinous amino acids with some exceptions. Amino acids are basically compounds containing nitrogen, hydrogen, oxygen, and carbon. They are founding elements of a protein chain. The proteins are the major factor in repairing the damaged cells, regenerating the dead ones, and control several other body functions. The neurotransmitters or simply the chemical messengers actually pass on the prompted message among the brain cells by bringing that impulse or electrochemical message to the brain cells of a respective brain region through a process called *endocytosis (bringing inside the cell).*

The intricacies involved neurotransmission is actually quite easy to understand when pictured like this: Several milkmen carrying bottles of milk exit the dairy farm. Every milkman has a destination where he must drop the milk by the door. He also has a known path to follow while dropping it off. This way all the bottles are delivered to the respective destinations by each milkman and a network is formed. This network remains connected with known and repeated parts unless a new client books an order for daily milk delivery or an old client shifts to a new place or cancels the delivery. This way new connections are formed, old ones are discarded, or reconnected in a different pattern. We may call the milk as an electrochemical message, milkman as a neuro transmitting messages carrying the electrochemical message, destination doorstep as a neuron receptor, traveling roads or pathways as synapses.

Back in Chinese ancient medicine, scholars used to research a lot on the effects of toxic food and drugs on the performance of mind and body. That is why detoxifying drinks became so popular. People began to believe in the wonders of chemicals and their effect on the well-being of both the mind and the body.

Many unusual methods were devised and many unique remedies were discovered to cure mental illnesses. Some supplements were purely devised to increase immunity and mental power such as Azoth. This universal medication or antidote was considered an invaluable concoction generally afforded by only the rich. Many variable accounts could be found in history describing its mysterious ingredients. It is also a famous element mentioned in alchemical studies.

Knowing your genetic history and the prevalent diseases in the family can also help you identify which foods are going to help you and which of them will have an adverse effect on you. , Moreover, age is not just a number here, it can be a deciding factor as well, so it can be the weight.

These things definitely affect how you behave and what will work for you.

Emotions as Biochemicals

Later it was discovered that even our emotions and feelings are the byproduct of biochemical reactions inside our body. To understand this concept, we would need to understand that there are two types of chemical releasing organs in our body called glands. The first type is the glands that secrete chemicals on the medial surface such as lacrimal glands (tears' secreting glands) or the glands that release chemicals on the outer surface such as sebaceous gland (sweat secreting glands). The second type is the glands that secrete chemicals inside the body, directly releasing them in the bloodstream. These sort of glands normally secrete chemical enzymes which have catalytic properties to speed up the biochemical processes happening inside the body systems. an example of these enzyme secreting glands are pancreas and liver that secrete enzymes to help in digestion but they may also secrete chemicals or hormones like insulin and other growth triggering hormones to aid in metabolism.

Other hormone-secreting glands are thyroid and pituitary glands which help in releasing the necessary chemicals such as thyroxin and oxytocin to name a few. These hormones travel in the blood, reaching the cells, stimulating the responses needed in several growth and maintenance functions of the body. They also are the reason why we experience responses like happiness, excitement, depression, love, passion, and emotional warmth.

Take *Oxytocin* for instance; known as a culprit behind an urge to cuddle and love, this hormone is released when you intimately socialize with someone and hug your friends or family members. Similarly, when you experience a sudden fear, shock, or rush of excitement, it is actually due to the release of *adrenaline* hormone secreted by adrenaline glands that are part of your nervous system. They produce a sort of urgent response in an emergency situation also known as *flight or fight* response.

Another instance can be considered to review your emotions as biochemicals; you have often heard that eating chocolate makes you happy.

Is it a myth? or a proven fact?

Actually, there is a chemical famously known as being both a neurotransmitter and a hormone called *serotonin.* This wondrous chemical substance is not only a regulating element for sleep, mood balance, social behavior, appetite, and sexual activity, but it also a definite memory enhancer. All the mystery lies in altering its present level in the body. Too much decline in the serotonin levels may cause depression or stress while too much increase may attribute to panic disorders and anxiety. Dark chocolate and bananas are said to be a mood lifter as they help produce serotonin. But too many bananas can induce diarrhea as well, why? Because due to an increase in serotonin, muscle activity in the stomach also increases and over digestion occurs, thus causing diarrhea.

We will discuss the issue of dark chocolate, caffeine, and their relation to serotonin in the upcoming pages separately. So, let us commence the detailed listing of major brain-boosting bounties one by one:

1. **Omega 3 Sources:**

There is a wealth of research available that proves the benefits of consuming food sources that are rich in omega 3. Modern statistical data has shown several positive results in the improvement of memory aspects such as spatial awareness by controlling the intake of Omega 3 supplements.

Omega 3 is the collection of three most important fatty acids i.e. AlA, EPA, and DHA. They control various functions of the body due to their important role in the central nervous system. To explain it more simply, a fatty acid is a molecule of fat or lipid, just like an oil molecule, composed of carbon and hydrogen molecular chains structured in a complex bonding. It is mainly derived from plant oils, animal fat, and is present naturally in our body too as part of lipid composition. These molecules, however, cannot be easily synthesized inside the brain and are generally required to be obtained from nutritional sources and supplements.

Essential sources of Omega 3 include:

✓ *Fish, particularly a fatty one:* Salmon, Anchovy, Sardine, Mackerel, Trout, Tuna, Albacore, Pilchard, etc. are some of the notable examples. Fish is considered to be one of the staples in the brain-food list, it helps in the regeneration of nervous tissues containing brain cells. By boosting brain development, it improves memory and helps in avoiding memory disorders such as Alzheimer or Dementia.

Historical pieces of evidence dating back to 1997, shows the result of an observation spanning three years. A group of old age men in the Netherlands was measured for their cognitive development levels and a significant decline was witnessed in those that used to consume less fish. Further longitudinal studies showed a decisive decline in brainpower for those having a low intake of Omega 3- rich diet.

- ✓ <u>*Cocoa Butter:*</u> It is a derived fat compound from seeds or beans of the cocoa plant. It is a vegetable oil, rich in omega 3 fatty acids. While the extract of these seeds is utilized as oil or butter, the pulp of the fruit containing these seeds is later used as cocoa or coffee. The cocoa liquor consisting of cocoa butter and finely ground particles of roasted cocoa beans plays a major part in the composition of the chocolate. The presence of cocoa butter in chocolate also helps it in melting easily.

- ✓ <u>*Shea Butter:*</u> It is a beautiful, ivory-colored oil that remains solid at room temperature. It is extracted from a plant species generally found in Africa called shea tree. Mostly used for beauty purposes, it can sometimes be substituted for cocoa butter if it is of food-grade quality.

✓ *Nuts, especially walnuts, chestnuts, water chestnut, and other:* Containing high content of DHA, one of the three Omega-3 fatty acids, nuts are a healthy food choice when it comes to memory improvement. Much like a computer, your brain's performance depends upon the number of instructions it can process in one cycle of activity. This can be accelerated through increased concentration and speed which is induced by various types of nuts.

✓ *Seeds such as flax seeds, perilla, chia, and other:* Also called the miracle seeds, these healthy seeds can fatty acids, nutritional fiber, and antioxidants that help in digestion, relaxation, and elimination of stress.

Flax seeds are said to be a major help in the reduction of the tumor. The seeds that are rich in ALA, can also decrease the potential risks of a heart attack. Perilla both as a seed and leaf has been used to treat various illnesses in Chinese medicine. It is known for its antidepressant and anti-inflammatory properties. Some brain training methods use perilla oil for inducing brain power and memory energization, preventing cognitive impairment.

✓ *Eggs:* Eggs are a powerful source of vitamins, minerals, protein, and healthy fats. Choline in the eggs can help in the composition of neurochemicals and enhance brain activity. The protein-rich content can also help in increasing the immunity and boosting the defense mechanism of the body.

✓ *Avocados:* This tasty, fleshy fruit can be a real brain booster due to its richness of caloric fat and fiber content. But watch out the size of portions in which you consume it as a small daily portion could go a long way depending on your requirement. Due to their *good fat* content, Avocados are often known as a superfood.

✓ *Seaweed:* Belonging to one of the various algae groups, seaweed can be a perfect alternative to meat for a vegetarian diet. Rich in proteins, minerals, and omega 3, it is a uniquely healthy choice for both mental and physical health.

✓ *Fish oil such as cod liver oil:* Being a supplement that is derived from codfish, this omega 3- rich oil also contains nutritious vitamins A, and D which help in brain health. The supplement can be consumed as a medicinal capsule too.

✓ *Other vegetable oils such as coconut oil, soybean oil, etc.:* Coconut oil is a major part of a ketogenic diet, the fats in the oil convert to ketones after breaking down and help energize the brain. For years, it has been used as a head relaxant massage oil also effective in hair growth. Soybean oil can be a good vegan substitute for fish oil.

2. **Sesame seeds:** Although sesame contains a little or no omega-3 fatty acids, they are rich in omega 6. They also contain a high content of iron, calcium, and fiber which give them a nutty, crunchy taste. Memory reconstruction is often said to be one of the many advantages of sesame seeds. People even use sesame

oil as a muscular pain relaxant and hair growth supplement. Tyrosine present in the sesame seeds helps in fighting depression and anxiety, revitalizing the brain activity.

3. **Carrot:** Carrot is always attributed to eyesight sharpener that also aids in strengthening the intellect by activating the cognitive processes. What actually happens is, carrot contains a type of compound that can also be found in some other herbal plants including chamomile, celery, rosemary, etc. This compound namely; *"luteolin"*, is notable for preventing nervous inflammation and memory decline. This compound is also present in olive oil. Earlier research experiments conducted on mice showed the positive effects of luteolin in young species that were subjected to a luteolin-rich diet. They exhibited improved memory and spatial awareness after the decreased risk of brain inflammation. Carrot's nutritional benefits can also be

obtained by consuming the roasted carrot seeds as an evening snack.

4. **Bottle Gourd Seeds:** Also known as calabash or long melon, this nutrient-rich food source is considered to be mind-and-heart healthy. Cultivated as a vine and used as a vegetable, it can provide multiple astonishing benefits to its consumers. Its white flesh along with the seeds contain a type of neuro transmitting chemical called choline which can improve the mental functionality. By maintaining the to the brain, it enhances the memorization and recall. It contributes to heart health by maintaining high cholesterol levels and preventing hypertension. This in result eliminates stress and depressive feelings and helps in regaining the lost focus.

5. **Sunflower seeds:** Being an excellent source of Vitamin B complex, Sunflower seeds are important to nervous health. The mineral content of these seeds includes adequate amounts of magnesium, potassium, calcium, and iron, etc. All of these help in regularizing or boosting the nervous system.

Sunflower seeds are also a great serotonin-level enhancer and help in improving the memory.

6. **Licorice:** Licorice root has a sweet, tangy taste. This woody supplement can be greatly beneficial in relieving the throat ache and increasing speech power. The licorice is thought to be a mind-sharpener by some experts due to the presence of a compound called carbenoxolone. This compound was tested on a group of people intent on improving their brain performance. The oral pill containing the compound was given to them as a dietary supplement but they thought it to be a miracle medicine due to the placebo effect. After a month, they showed signs of sharpened vocal skills and articulation. Their communication skills and literal memory also improved considerably. More tests were carried out on diabetic patients as well. They appeared to have developed a noticeable fluency in wordiness and textual remembrance. Licorice is often available at herbal stores in the form

of powdered supplement or small wooden sticks which can be suckled on like a lollipop.

7. **Spanish Cherry or Bulletwood:** Botanically called *Mimusops elengi,* Spanish cherries are native to Asia and northern part of Australia. These are edible fruit of an evergreen tree species often used as an effective herbal remedy for various ailments. Its leaves are a popular cure for headache and other mental disorders in Ayurvedic medicine.

8. **Black Pepper:** Most common of the various seasonings and spices, black pepper contains *piperine* which can be a powerful brain booster. Research shows that piperine has a positive effect on the improvement of the immune system and memory skills.

9. **Chickpeas:** Loaded with proteins and minerals such as magnesium, chickpeas can be an energizing supplement for the mind. Accelerating the transfer of signals across nervous pathways, the nutrients in the

beans or chickpeas, helps the brain to respond more quickly.

10. **Dark Chocolate:** In recent centuries, the hype about the chocolate and its positive relation to health has been towering. Research after research has been conducted to unveil the mysteries behind chocolate, preferably dark chocolate. People are euphoric about dark chocolate's rich color, flavorful taste, and gratifying aftertaste. Obtained from the cocoa tree as mentioned earlier, the cocoa beans are roasted and ground then a mixture of these ground beans, cocoa butter, and sweetener etc. is concocted. This way it all transforms into a yummy chocolate bar that is rich in minerals, chemicals like serotonin, and other antioxidants. Unsweetened variety of chocolate, taken in moderate amounts can be a healthier choice.

The high percentage of magnesium present in cocoa helps in smooth transmission of nervous impulses or electrochemical messages, thus boosting the brain activity exponentially. About the relation of chocolate ith serotonin, much has been the subject of research an much is still open for debate. As the neurologists suggest that serotonin levels in the brain cannot be altered by serotonin being produced or consumed in the gut, this means that the brain must maintain its own range of serotonin. Chocolate or its parent source; cocoa beans, help in increasing the levels of this neuro transmitting chemical serotonin in the brain. Cocoa also helps in maintaining the blood flow to the brain, hence accelerating the brain activity.

Like many other plant-derived foods and supplements including fruits and vegetables, chocolate also contains pigments called flavonoids. These molecular compounds help in detoxification of the brain and the body. They are called antioxidants because they eliminate free oxygen radicals or ions found in the bloodstream which may cause harm to the cells and hindrance to their regular functioning. However, food scientists suggest that flavonoids may surpass ordinary antioxidants in their added benefits such as; their behavior improvement properties and memory enhancement potential. So now you know, that dark, rich color of your chocolate bar is not just for show!

11.   **Coffee:** The main reason why coffee is always promoted as a mood enhancer or memory booster is because of the presence of caffeine in it. According to a neuroscientific research study, caffeine intake during a revision prior to an exam often result in better performance and result outcome. This is due to the discovery that caffeine help maintains and retains the learned information as a long-term memory. It blocks the sleep stimulating hormone and makes you more active, sharpening your thinking skills. However, it must be consumed in moderate quantity to improve cognition as coffee is also said to be a great help in preventing *MCI i.e. Mild Cognitive Impairment.*

12.   **Green tea:** Contrary to black coffee, green tea contains smaller amounts of caffeine. Instead its antioxidant properties, vitamin, and mineral-rich content, and anti-inflammation compounds complement the health further. According to research, all the components of the green tea when consumed together can provide a whole healthy uplifting to the

overall body functions. The polyphenols in the green tea when mixed with a little caffeine, can activate the short-term memory or working memory and help prevent cell degeneration.

13.   **Ginger:** Consisting of more than 90 nutritional compounds, half of which are antioxidants, ginger easily surpasses many other dietary supplements in providing amazing health benefits. By preventing inflammation in the brain and other body parts, it helps eliminate mental ailments such as Alzheimer's and brain fog. It also possesses anti-aging, anti and anti-depressant characteristics because it helps increase the levels of serotonin. It can help boost up the blood flow and improves the activity of glial cells and vagus nerve that is why it has been used to treat dementia as well. Glial cells are the most common type of brain cells found in the central nervous system. Although not active participants in nervous signal transmission, these supporting cells or cleaning agents play a vital role in the disposal of the dead cells' remains. Whereas thee vagus nerve is the connection between the brain and the body and handles several essential nervous functions. Those

having ginger extract as a supplementary medicine have been known to exhibit stronger critical thinking skills and longer attention span.

14.	**Ginseng:** Typically, a root of a plant called *Panax ginseng*, this superb herb is an invaluable health supplement. Popularized in traditional medicine as an all-in-one remedy for universal well-being, its cognitive benefits include increased brain activity and strong immunity. Ginseng can be taken as a leafy diet, in powdered form, or brewed as an herbal tea. It is considered to be a precious part of wild flora, to avoid risking extinction, some countries have strict laws against harvesting it illegally. Some states allow its cultivation and export though. Some apply conditions such as prohibiting the premature harvest and letting it grow for at least five years before collecting the crop. However, you can cultivate it in your own backyard legally and gain long term benefits. Common variants include Korean ginseng, American ginseng, and Chinese ginseng.

15.	**Ginko Biloba or Maidenhair Tree:** Due to its ancient history and millions of years of age, this popular tree is lovingly named as a *living fossil*. Its medicinal history dates back to early Chinese medicine. Accounts have been mentioned in renowned traditional medicine scriptures about its effect on preventing memory declination. However, modern studies deny any considerable effect on cognitive improvement. Still, the matter is of contradiction as several users of the herbal extract claim improvement and promoters of alternative medicine continue to present this as a memory-enhancing supplement. Regardless of the debate, no one can disagree with the fact that the herb is rich in antioxidants that eventually complements brain function due to their detoxifying properties.

16.   **Turmeric:** Also called lively spice and blood purifier, turmeric is a miraculous kitchen ingredient that can be used to treat various ailments. It contains a compound called *curcumin* that has brilliant anti-oxidation properties, it can lower the risk of Alzheimer as well. Curcumin extract can be available in separate

supplementary form as well which, if taken regularly, can improve the mood and the memory.

17.   **Blueberries:** This beautiful, colorful fruit is a treat to the eye. Berries' rich blue color is also due to the plant pigment called Flavonoids. As mentioned before, these antioxidants are not only a detoxifying factor in the biochemical processes of the body but also help in memory improvement.

18.   **Broccoli:** This nutrient-rich, leaf green vegetable is widely used across the globe. Revered by the health-conscious people, broccoli contains a high content of vitamin K and is also rich in neuro transmitting chemicals called Choline. Some benefits of Choline has been mentioned before as well. Here we will tell you an important reason for why Choline can be a brain booster. Actually, Choline is an essential factor in producing the neurotransmitter called *acetylcholine.* This chemical is the main

stimulator for increased functionality of memory, muscle, and behavior.

19.   **Spinach:** Rich in minerals such as magnesium, zinc, iron, and vitamins such as A, C, E, and K, spinach can help prevent memory decline and hypertension. As experts state the reason for low attention span and drowsiness is often due to iron deficiency. As a green vegetable comprising leafy flesh, it is also rich in dietary fiber that is needed for digestion and overall improved functionality of the body.

20.   **Indian Gooseberry or Amla:** Rich in vitamin C, various minerals such as phosphorus and calcium, fiber content, and antioxidants, Amla is a good source of brainpower. Often referred to as a super brain diet, the literal meaning of Amla in Sanskrit is: "the rejuvenator". It can be consumed both as a fruit and juice or energy drink. Even the oil extract from this

fruit, applied on the scalp as a massage tonic, works wonders for brain relaxation and hair growth.

Chapter 12: Practical Exercises and Fun Tests

Memory Mnemonics

Required Material for Exercises:

- A paper and a pen.

Exercise # 1:

Objective:

Consider the given information and make a suitable rhyming mnemonic for it to be easily remembered.

Information:

"There are about 118 chemical elements discovered until 2019. The periodic table is a brilliant way to represent these chemical elements and categorize them into groups and periods. This way their properties can be learned easily. The first published periodic table of Mendeleev was recognized in 1869. There are 7 horizontal rows in this tabular display called periods and 18 vertical columns called groups."

Exercise # 2:

Objective:

Read and arrange the following names of certain countries of Asia in order to create an easily memorable acronym mnemonic representing these countries appropriately.

Information:

"China, Pakistan, Bangladesh, Japan, Iran, India, Malaysia, Singapore, Vietnam, Myanmar, Philippines, Thailand, Afghanistan, Bahrain."

Exercise # 3:

Objective:

There are some pieces of information (a, b, c) given below. Using any of the learned effective mnemonic strategies such as legend lists, images, letter patters, concept maps, chunking methods, narration, association, link method, or color-coding, devise a suitable strategy to learn each of the following pieces of information. Note that your choice of mnemonic for each piece of information must correspond to the style of that information in order to facilitate the ease of remembrance and relevance of the memory technique used.

Information (a):

"The book we are discussing contains these concepts and ideas as its main theme. Natural herbs, Benefits of health maintenance, Vegetarian diet, botanical gardens in Asia, Effects of cocoa beans on health, Green tea as a herb, Herbal remedies, and products, etc."

Information (b):

"The traveling bag must include these 5 articles for any journey you are embarking on: 1) Clothes, 2)Dry Food, 3) A Spare Pair of Shoes, 4) Water-Proof Camera, 5) Money / ID Card Wallet."

Information (c):

"Human body's organ systems and each organ's function in detail."

--------------------------------*----------------*--------------
----

Fun Activity: Creating Your Own Memory Palace or Maze

Exercise # 4:

Required:

- A physically real, complex place. Clearly seen and mentally imaginable.
- A piece of information to be remembered.

Information to be Allocated and Stored:

"Answers to the expected questions of an upcoming viva. Such as:

Q1: What is the aim of learning?

Q2: What is meant by gender in Education?

Q3: How do you differentiate between Society and Community?

Q4: What are the different types of educational philosophies?

Q5: Why is learning soft skills more important than academics nowadays?

Q6: What is your opinion regarding the vocational training of the youngsters?

Q7: How can homeschooling lack in social development of a student?

Q8: Why is school considered a mini-society by John Dewey?

Q9: What is meant by Pragmatism in education?

Q10: How do you define the phrase: *Education for Life?*"

Objective & Method:

Select a familiar place to act as your physical memory storage or mind palace. Imagine this place in your mind. You must have seen it clearly beforehand to be able to visualize each nook and corner with clarity and detail. Arrange each answer of the viva questions to be allocated in a particular place in your memory palace. Use the method described in the memory improvement techniques earlier in this book.

------------------------------------*------------------*----
--------------*------------*

Daily Practice: Creating Your Own Memory Journal

Material:

- A journal or logbook to record daily entries.
- Some, pens, color highlighters, and markers.
- Some bookmarks and sticky notes.

Objective:

This practice is important to be regularly maintained in order to increase your memory retention and refreshing your acquired knowledge and life experiences.

Method:

- Select a time for your daily journaling, usually in the night. Try that this remains the same throughout your daily schedule. i.e. the exactness of the time slot daily will start habituating and alerting your inner clock after a few days. The mind will also start anticipating the refreshment of memories at that particular hour of the day.
- Reflect on the experiences of that day, think about them and recollect them in your mind.
- Make use of mnemonic devices such as word expression mnemonics, outlines, models, graphic

organizers, etc. to summarize the information and devise your own version of a shorthand strategy.

- Use highlighters and bookmarks wherever necessary to emphasize the importance of certain points.
- Use markers or sharpies for bolding and color-coding information in the journal entries.
- Revisit and refer to old entries whenever linkages are necessary or recollection is required. Also revise them on occasions just to keep your memories afresh.

Bonus: Homemade Brain booster Remedy

This amazing homemade recipe has garnered more results than even the most expensive medicinal supplements couldn't. The ingredients used in this brain booster are all easily available in our homes or local herb shop.

Ingredients:

- ✓ Fennel seeds: 1 cup
- ✓ Almonds: 1 cup
- ✓ The famous four seeds combination: 1 cup
    - *(Pumpkin seeds + Musk melon seeds + Watermelon seeds + Cucumber seeds)*
- ✓ Rock brown sugar or *Mishri*: 1/2 cup
- ✓ Roasted chickpeas: 1 & 1/2 cups
- ✓ Cashews, pistachios, and oatmeal: optional
- ✓ Milk: As required
- ✓ Honey: As required

Method of Preparation:

1. Grind together fennel, almonds, *four seeds' combination,* rock sugar, roasted chickpeas, and other nuts or oatmeal (if added), in a grinding machine until finely granulated or powdered.
2. Fill a medium-sized jar with this powdered supplement.
3. To make a serving, take a glass filled warm milk.
4. Add a tablespoon of honey in the milk and stir.
5. Now take a spoonful of the supplement from the jar and mix it with the honeyed milk, stir well.
6. Consume the brain booster this way, twice a day before breakfast in the morning and before sleeping at night time.

Note:

Daily intake of this twice can reveal significant improvement in memory retention and brain activity. It has been quite successful with school and college students and exam attempters. Those who memorize lengthy scriptures also found this recipe quite helpful in stimulating high response and sharpened memory.

Conclusion

Thank you for making it through to the end of *Memory Improvement*, let's hope it was informative and able to provide you with all of the tools you need to achieve your goals whatever they may be.

The next step is to start benefiting from the content presented to you and implementing the useful strategies discussed in this book. Most of us often close the books and along with that, close our *windows of opportunities* too. These windows of opportunities are our memories. Our senses absorb the surrounding impressions and store the knowledge as memories. The book you just read may or may not have increased your knowledge but it sure has emphasized some useful points and concepts. At least you have made some new memories and revived some old ones.

Most of us have experienced that crucial moment when you are about to say something to someone and just as you grab their attention, you forget what you were about to say. These sorts of issues make you all the more eager to learn and implement helpful techniques for memory improvement. The learning has started as you began reading this book or similar books on this topic, now is the time for active practice. The path to actual improvement and implementation starts where the book reading finishes. Now is the time for real work.

Before the final note, we are leaving you with a quick self-question:

Are you a memory decliner, memory retainer or memory improver?

Finally, if you found this book useful in any way, a review on Amazon is always appreciated!

www.ingramcontent.com/pod-product-compliance
Lightning Source LLC
Chambersburg PA
CBHW061755250726
48657CB00001B/130